Jacques Rancière and the Politics of Art Cinema

Jacques Rancière and the Politics of Art Cinema

James Harvey

EDINBURGH
University Press

Edinburgh University Press is one of the leading university presses in the UK. We publish academic books and journals in our selected subject areas across the humanities and social sciences, combining cutting-edge scholarship with high editorial and production values to produce academic works of lasting importance. For more information visit our website: edinburghuniversitypress.com

Edinburgh University Press Ltd
The Tun – Holyrood Road
12 (2f) Jackson's Entry
Edinburgh EH8 8PJ

First published in hardback by Edinburgh University Press 2018

Typeset in 11/13 Monotype Ehrhardt by
Servis Filmsetting Ltd, Stockport, Cheshire

A CIP record for this book is available from the British Library

ISBN 978 1 4744 2378 6 (hardback)
ISBN 978 1 4744 6293 8 (paperback)
ISBN 978 1 4744 2379 3 (webready PDF)
ISBN 978 1 4744 2380 9 (epub)

Contents

Figures

Acknowledgements

The shape of this book has taken on many guises in the six years of its writing. It is fair to say that, through this process, I have come to appreciate the limits of, and potentialities for, cinema's ability to *do* politics. For helping me articulate my ideas, I must offer the greatest thanks to Tina Kendall: the best doctoral supervisor anyone could ever hope for.

Along the way, I have also been lucky enough to receive the friendly critical attention of: Richard Rushton, Tanya Horeck, Martin O'Shaughnessy, Bill Marshall, Angelos Koutsourakis, Shohini Chaudhuri, William Brown, Sarah Wright, Geoffrey Kantaris, Nike Jung, Aaron Hunter, Matilda Mroz, Tiago de Luca, Miriam de Rosa, Simon Payne, Rosalind Galt, Colin Wright, and Joss Hands, as well as many vital contributions from those kind enough to attend numerous talks I have given over the past few years.

This book is for my two sons, Joseph and Joshua.

Introduction: Politics and Art Cinema

We know too well that the systemic social violences of inequality are social, historical and economic; that they are so immanently perceivable shows that they are aesthetic also. Who is seen and heard; who speaks and who is spoken to; in what ways one can communicate and how one experiences communication: these issues are still rigidly determined by hierarchies enshrined in tradition and are intensified more than ever in twenty-first-century global capitalism. The aesthetic is the philosophical category describing experience and perception and, as such, it plays a fundamental role in articulating how we experience a social life. The aesthetics of politics must, therefore, play a central role in challenging the mechanics of each social life. As a category of cinema most routinely and self-consciously described as 'aesthetic', art films provide acute spaces for the acting out of these challenges. This book is an attempt to shed light on the political potential of art cinema today. My hope is that if we contemplate carefully some notable works of global art cinema in the twenty-first century, we may delineate in the films an extra-textual engagement with the social malaise in which we find ourselves at present. Geographically and stylistically disparate, the films analysed in this book provide diverse and novel responses to issues that are often global in nature. Even in their social and historical contexts, each of the films discussed allows us to engage with a concept as familiar in sound as it is alien in reality: politics. The aim of this book, therefore, is to argue that such a thing as politics exists in contemporary art cinema.

DEFINING POLITICS

Few thinkers have had more inspiring, innovative things to say about the politics of aesthetics in recent years than Jacques Rancière. Two points made by Rancière in *Disagreement* (1999) – his seminal text on political philosophy – have provided the inspiration for the arguments made herein. The first regards the way we conceive of politics. For Rancière, it is a word that has been over-assigned; that has been near emptied of its radical historical promise of change and flux; and, as such, has been made synonymous with the day jobs of elected representatives: the people who, supposedly, *do* politics. However, these people are not *doing* politics at all. Rather, for Rancière, the activities of state politicians are far more likely to represent something at odds with the actual occurrence of politics: order. Those charged with the responsibility of doing politics on behalf of the people represent an instrument of power that ultimately works to consolidate order, reinforce the appearance of politics in 'civilised society' and, in turn, play a starring role in determining how we experience social life. Taking up Rancière's position on this matter, I assume an alternative thesis: politics runs against orderly society in its defining nature. Politics is not an activity that protects the dispossessed or preserves order – it is interruptive:

> The struggle between the rich and the poor is not social reality, which politics then has to deal with. It is the actual institution of politics itself. There is politics when there is a part of those who have no part, a part or party of the poor. Politics does not happen just because the poor oppose the rich. It is the other way around: politics (that is, the interruption of the simple effects of domination by the rich) causes the poor to exist as an entity. The outrageous claim of the demos to be the whole of the community only satisfies in its own way – that of a *party* – the requirement of politics. Politics exists when the natural order of domination is interrupted by the institution of a part of those who have no part. (Rancière 1999: 11)

Laying firm foundations for a strict, Greek definition of politics, Rancière immediately sets himself up in opposition to many of the key political thinkers of the twentieth century. One might spend time delineating the difference between this mode of thinking politics from conservative thinkers such as Leo Strauss or Carl Schmitt; the liberalism of Max Weber or Karl Popper; or the revised Marxisms of the 1970s, from which Rancière's own early thought derived and detached itself. However, such is the currency of Rancière in contemporary philosophical discourse, several fine texts have already achieved this feat.[1] One key difference I shall briefly make clear, though, is from his teacher, Louis Althusser. In Althusser, politics concerns the historical contest between two distinct social groupings: between the working classes and 'the political representatives of the ruling classes in possession of State power' (Althusser 1969: 100). If we read Althusser through Rancière, politics appears to have been torn from its essential interruptive activity performed by those who have no part in society. It is mounted instead onto a customised scene of class struggle. Rancière's break with Althusser concerned this very dispute – a disagreement regarding who has the capacity and social positioning to utter politically. As he argues in *Althusser's Lesson* (2011a), Althusser spoke *on behalf of* the people, from the position of an intellectual. There is a clear way of differentiating the meaning of politics for Rancière from the common usage of *a politics*. There is no such thing as 'a politics'; politics is a concept with its own predetermined activities and functions, which can be described as the interruption of the social order by those excluded from it, in turn expressing the existence of a 'part of those who have no part'.

The interruptive moment of politics cannot be provided from above. We must assume, then, with Rancière, that politics can only derive from the sites occupied by parties excluded from society ('the part of those who have no part'). He makes this very point in *Disagreement*:

> Politics . . . actually happens very little or rarely. What is usually lumped together under the name of political history or political science in fact stems more often than not from other mechanisms concerned with holding on to the exercise of majesty, the curacy of divinity, the command of armies, and the management of interests. Politics only occurs when these mechanisms are stopped in their tracks . . . (Rancière 1999: 17)

Politics exists solely in these rare instances of interruption: this is a bold claim. We would have to assume that most of the things we tend to consider political (elections, protests, debate, subversive actions) are by no means political in and of themselves. Rather, read this way, these very actions might indeed be seen to reinforce the existing social order. To differentiate between these mechanisms of power and politics proper, Rancière uses the term, 'police'. The term police, or 'policing', has two important precedents in twentieth-century French political theory: Althusser's 'hailing' police who interpellate in the name of the state apparatus (Althusser 1971) and the disciplinary regime of Michel Foucault's panopticon (Foucault 1975). Rancière's usage signals his closeness to Foucault and his difference from Althusser. Following Foucault, policing for Rancière regards the distribution of bodies in a community (Rancière 1999: 280); it can occur 'as much from the spontaneity of social relations as from the rigidity of state functions' (ibid.: 29). Not simply the name for institutions of oppression, policing exists throughout each social environment: from military bodies, to the arrangement of streets, to the way one dresses and speaks. What Althusser attached wholly to ideology, Rancière challenges in the name of some potential spontaneity.

> The police is thus first an order of bodies that defines the allocation of ways of doing, ways of being, and ways of saying, and sees that those bodies are assigned by name to a particular place and task; it is an order of the visible and the sayable that sees that a particular activity is visible and another is not, that this speech is understood as discourse and another as noise . . . I now propose to reserve the term politics for an extremely determined activity antagonistic to policing . . . (Rancière 1999: 29)

With Rancière, politics does not relate to the upholding or undermining of police orders; it involves a rupture – an event that is not only at odds with a specific law, but that threatens the authority of law in general. By way of illustration, Rancière has raised the useful example of Rosa Parks's rejection of the back seat of the bus in Montgomery, in 1955 (Rancière 2006b: 61). More than just a singular moment of rebellion, Parks's crime was constitutive of a greater challenge to social apartheid, which has in turn played a significant role in the cultural opposition to racism ever since. Social movements arise from, and are consolidated by, these rare political events. The stakes of such antagonism are such that these kinds of occurrence are far greater in the long term than they may appear at first sight. To view the state of a society at any one time is to glance only at a surface that conceals a greater, historical, policing process. Politics interrupts these processes. It makes visible a sight previously hidden from clear view. The Parks example is such an effective one since its racial context provides one of the most direct evocations of the aesthetics of politics: it challenges an order of the visible. In a racist police order, one's role in society is determined by appearance alone. To cross over between these policed sites is to contravene the order and, subsequently, to throw into disarray such a social order. The continuing existence of this racist police order is demonstrative of the difficulty of realising fully the potential of political interruption. Yet, terms like 'democracy' and 'equality' are still being used and abused. Since systems of apartheid have been dismantled and greater rights afforded to each sex and sexuality, leaders of liberal democracies have taken it upon themselves to attach the contemporary police order to the high point of Western civilisation. This argument gained force at the end of the 1980s with the decline of Communism in Eastern Europe, which, for Francis Fukuyama, brought with it 'the end of history' (1992). Apparently today's global, free-market capitalism is the inevitable destination for modernity. Rancière defines this conception of society as a regime of 'consensus'.

> What consensus means, in effect, is not people's agreement amongst themselves but the matching of sense with sense: the accord made between a sensory regime of the presentation of things and a mode of interpretation of their meaning. The consensus governing us is a machine

> of power insofar as it is a machine of vision. It claims to observe merely that which we can all see in aligning two propositions about the state of the world: one maintains that we have come at last to live in times of peace; the other states the condition of that peace – that there is no more than what there is. (Rancière 2010: viii)

Consensus is an inherently aesthetic idea. As 'a sensory regime of the presentation of things and a mode of interpretation of their meaning', it is not essentially bound to specific sociological contexts; it relates rather more abstractly to modes of experience and perception. Nevertheless, since an accord is made between presentation and interpretation, consensus relates precisely to the postmodern malaise proclaimed by Fukuyama and reviled by leftist philosophers since. Consensus functions by way of accounting for meaning on impact: we need not question what we see, for the world just *is* as it appears. This is paradoxically reassuring and unnerving. One need not probe the surfaces for deeper meaning for things just are as they appear. Yet, insofar as things just *are*, nothing else is thereby possible. Consensus politics works by reproducing uniform social configurations and eliminating the possibility of reconfigurative interruption – it anaesthetises political activity. The development of a 'centre ground' over the past three decades has been the defining achievement of consensus. Everything that challenges it appears extreme. However, the prevailing regime of centrism is beginning to crumble, due to the rise of nationalism and the widespread embrace of organised neo-fascist organisations. How are we to understand Rancière's political philosophy in this context? Do we still live in times of consensus?

While proclamations of grand historical change abound in this climate, it is clear that Rancière's idea of consensus remains. What else do the twenty-first-century far right represent if not an even more radical 'matching of sense with sense'? All the answers offered by the nationalist groups across the Western world rely upon positing an accord 'between a sensory regime of the presentation of things and a mode of interpretation of their meaning'. While in the late twentieth century this accord involved the association of free-market economic policy with social prosperity and the association of human otherness with threat, the accord today involves a radical – perhaps wholesale – embrace of the latter. The foreign has become the category most frequently deployed by these new consensual formations in order to solidify a machine of power, to reassure people of their well-being, to remind them of their dependence upon it, to further marginalise the part of those who have no part and to extend the reach of inequality. Rancière's claim that the very definition of politics is something to be reassessed is enormously important since it concerns the possibility of progressive change in times of apparent tyranny.

POLITICAL AESTHETICS AND CINEMA

While Rancière's writing marks a major intervention into contemporary political thought, it can also be read in line with a history of political philosophy in general.[2] We can locate him in a lineage of thinkers who seek to articulate the aesthetic dimension of politics and, in turn, begin to understand how the politics of works of art can be examined. Rancière's principal philosophical reference points include Romantic philosophers such as Immanuel Kant, August Schlegel and Friedrich Schiller, whose Romantic conceptions of play and imagination were bound to utopian political futures. Kant's aesthetic principle of subjective universality provides a seed of democracy in our everyday, lived experiences (Kant [1790] 2000). For Schiller, 'aesthetic communication alone unites society, because it applies to what is common to all its members' (Schiller [1794] 2004: 189). Rancière returns to this Romantic ideal of emancipation deriving from imagination and experience, in order to turn not away from society, but more creatively towards it. Political change can only arise from some form of aesthetic reconfiguration of one's environment. As such, one must engage and be engaged by one's imagination. He recovers such ideas in a contemporary vein through what he terms the 'distribution of the sensible' (2004): an 'implicit law governing the sensible order that parcels out places and forms of participation in a common world' (ibid.: 89). We have seen already something akin to the distribution of the sensible in the earlier concept of policing. In *The Politics of Aesthetics*, however, Rancière is concerned with placing the aesthetic dimension in the foreground. Building on the interruptive politics described in *Disagreement*, politics is here defined as: 'a delimitation of spaces and times, of the visible and the invisible, of speech and noise, that simultaneously determines the place and the stakes of politics as a form of experience' (Rancière, 2004: 13). Focusing on the sensory dimension of politics develops further how we might come to delineate, analyse and perhaps act upon future action. Taken together, *Disagreement* and *The Politics of Aesthetics* provide a rich template for understanding 'politics as a form of experience'. Precise and determinable qualities are presented that allow us to pinpoint the occurrence of politics describable through the terms of art: politics 'revolves around what is seen and what can be said about it, around who has the ability to see and the talent to speak, around the properties of spaces and the possibilities of time' (ibid.) Who is making or viewing sights and sounds? Who occupies the light and the dark? A political aesthetics of cinema can be broached on these very terms.

The turn towards aesthetic philosophy more directly in the later work provides Rancière a space to offer some novel analyses in the fields of literature (2011b), cinema (2006a; 2014b) and modernist art in general (2013). Carried through many of his textual analyses is a keen eye for locating what he has called a 'suitable political work of art' (2004: 63), which is deemed suitable since it disrupts 'the relationship between the visible, the sayable and the thinkable without having to use the terms of the message as a vehicle' (2004: 63). Unpacking this statement will go a long way towards understanding the politics of art cinema. First, we have a familiar reference to the disruption of the visible, the sayable and the thinkable: that is, the distribution of the sensible. For art to function politically, Rancière argues, our existing knowledge must be challenged in some way. However, this is only half the solution: how do we reconcile the political art without 'the terms of the message'?

Political art should not explain to its spectator, but, rather, should provide a space of engagement for the spectator to occupy and participate. This distinguishes Rancière from many twentieth-century political aestheticians, for whom politics was a quality determined by the level of overt agitation on the surface of the text. His dispute with this approach is raised in *The Emancipated Spectator* (2009c), which helps us further appreciate what is being claimed in *The Politics of Aesthetics*. *The Emancipated Spectator* is a critique of aesthetic theories describing the active and passive spectator. One key target is the Brechtian tradition of alienation, whereby the viewer is apparently jolted into a sustained intellectual relationship with the performance. Classical conventions of narrative, linearity and identification are challenged in the work of Brecht. The spectator thereby becomes aware of the artifice of the performance and, it is hoped, of the world around her. However, while the intention is to champion an equality of intelligence and invite the spectator into the making of meaning, instead 'the spectator is discredited because she does nothing, whereas actors on the stage or workers outside put their bodies in action' (ibid.: 12). Countering the Brechtian paradigm that assumes an initially passive spectatorship, Rancière claims that 'emancipation begins when we . . . understand that viewing is also an action that transforms or confirms the distribution of positions' (ibid.: 13).

Rancière's opposition to these forms of political aesthetics can also be applied to film theory, offering a critique of what Sylvia Harvey called 'political modernism' (1982). In her important article that would serve to provide the impetus for a number of critiques of 1970s film theory thereafter,[3] Harvey recognised this stultifying address of the spectator. She argued that political modernists 'tended to assume that texts could be defined as "radical" on the basis of stylistic properties alone, rather than on the basis of the tripartite relationship between textual properties, contemporary social reality and historically formed readers' (Harvey 1982: 51). Thus, from Laura Mulvey's attempts to imagine cinema as a 'political weapon' that might overcome patriarchal thinking (1975: 6) to Colin MacCabe's reading of Jean-Luc Godard's films (1985), political cinema is said to awaken spectators from the illusory cinema of classical narrative techniques. While committed to confronting systems of hegemony in and through film, these works insist on speaking down to the spectator. *The Emancipated Spectator* offers an alternative position. As with the fate of the radical left in the 1970s, we might speculate that the inevitable impasse of political modernism is more to do with the contempt often expressed by critical voices towards the people they claim to represent. In response to these 'embodied allegories of inequality' (Rancière 2009c: 12), Rancière champions an emancipated spectator for whom 'viewing is also an action that confirms or transforms this redistribution of positions' (ibid.: 13). If, then, we want to theorise a political aesthetics of cinema today, this may hinge upon defying interpretive limitation or (anti-)ideological formal strategies of political modernism.

To return to *The Politics of Aesthetics*, Rancière argues against 'the terms of the message' in order to challenge the stultifying logic of political modernism. This does not mean that political art must not have a point to make. On the contrary, political art, he says, 'would ensure, at one and the same time . . . the readability of the message that threatens to destroy the sensible form of art and the radical uncanniness that threatens to destroy all political meaning' (Rancière 2004: 63). The sensible order installed by the artwork is hereby redistributed on two fronts. Political art should first be socially engaged enough to deny infinite interpretive frames; but it should also be formally inventive enough to disrupt determined social narratives. The example he uses to illustrate is Roberto Rossellini's *Europe '51* (1952). Rancière locates in this film a way of staging a stylistic clash: between a socially conscious message of democracy and an inventive play with cinematic form, seemingly threatening the clarity of this message. The police order examined in *Europe '51* is post-fascist Italy: a time of rigid social division, whereby shared endeavour towards a common, post-war humanity is apparently helpless to overcome the economic gap. As I have detailed elsewhere (Harvey-Davitt 2014), Rancière's locating of political potential in the film relates to a simultaneous thematic and stylistic interruption. Rossellini's neorealist style provides an artistic distribution of the sensible, thwarted at various moments in the film through the momentary breaks from realist conventions of editing, lighting, and performance (Figure I.1). That Rancière makes his bold assertion on the politics of art through a film demonstrates the centrality of cinema to his political aesthetic ideas in general. However, while the aforementioned appears to provide a critical toolbox for dissecting the politics of cinema, the more recent *The Intervals of Cinema* (2014b) directly counters such an idea:

> There is no politics of cinema, there are singular forms that filmmakers use to connect the two meanings of the word 'politique' which can be used to describe a fiction in general and a cinematic fiction in particular: politics in what a film is saying – the history of a movement or conflict,

Figure I.1 The aesthetic shock of Irene's arrival at the factory in *Europe '51*.

> exposure of a situation of suffering or injustice – and something more like 'policy', meaning the specific strategy of an artistic approach. (ibid: 104)

If we place 'politics' as it is described in Rancière's more abstract engagements with art in conversation with the 'politics' from his writing on cinema, we may question how he comes to deny a politics of cinema. How does he come to replace it with this watered-down, dual alternative, of *politique*? The notion of a *politique* of cinema is most commonly associated with the *politique des auteurs*: a mode of film criticism associated with the French New Wave. The auteur theory (as it became known in the anglophone world) described a way of approaching film that holds no explicit or implicit relation to any political philosophy. It was a way of approaching film with a centre of meaning occupied by the director: film as art and filmmakers as artists. By conceiving of the politics of cinema in an auteurist vein, then, in the space of a few sentences, Rancière's view of the political potential of art becomes altogether detached from the medium of cinema. Since his other writings on the politics of aesthetics conceive of politics as contingent upon the properties of space and the possibilities of time, I would like to use Rancière's other writings to challenge this assertion and suggest instead that we can conceive of a politics of cinema. In the twentieth century, no medium was more revolutionary in its reconfiguration of spatial properties and temporal possibilities. From the masses convening in the cinema to view early moving images, to underground gatherings rebelling against censorship, films, spectators and cinemas have provided a major source of collective agitation against normative social orders. Why does Rancière leap so boldly to the conclusion that there is no politics of cinema? Do distributions of the sensible not exist in the making and sharing of films? And do these distributions of the sensible not capacitate a form of politics – a 'politics of cinema' – in their own right? Moreover, do cinema's distributions of the sensible not foreshadow political activities outside of the cinema space? These are questions I am seeking to answer throughout my analyses. For now, in order to elaborate on my dispute with Rancière's dismissal of a politics of cinema, I shall revisit three engagements with films that rehearse his two uses of *politique*.

My first example concerns his most overt engagement with a politics of cinema, from his first book-length study of cinema, *Film Fables* (2006a). Approaching Jean-Luc Godard's *La Chinoise* (1967), Rancière argues that the film constructs a dual *politique* of Marxist philosophy: 'Godard puts "cinema" between two Marxisms – Marxism as a matter of representation, and Marxism as the principle of representation' (Rancière 2006a: 143). Throughout the essay, it is always concluded that *La Chinoise* offers the semblance of Marxian political theory: 'Godard shows us what the words and gestures of politics looks like' (ibid. 151). He praises Godard's representation of Maoist scission through film form, but restricts its achievement to the construction of a story. It is, in other words, a useful illustration of what he has elsewhere called 'metapolitics': 'the discourse on the falseness of politics' (Rancière 1999: 82). Godard's Marxism is the epitome of metapolitics – a self-reflexive mode that both deconstructs the lie of the social (the uncovering of ideological interpellation, in Althusser's terms) and reconstructs the social with the broken fragments: in other words, we go from the idea that class is a social construction to the principle that there is one true class. For Rancière, in its deconstruction and reconstruction of society, *La Chinoise* is exemplary of the metapolitics of cinema and its essential inability to realise politics proper. Throughout his work, Rancière seems to reserve an air of hostility for Godard. Mark Robson has suggested that this may be due to the apparent convergences and shared intellectual histories of the two, which Rancière is thereafter at pains to dismiss (Robson 2013: 134). Robson's recognition of the shared philosophical backgrounds and contrasting destinations of Rancière and Godard demands a review of a second example – one less bound to the contested ground of post-'68 Marxism and conversant instead with more recent debates.

In 'The ethical turn of aesthetics and politics' (2010: 184–204), Rancière broaches the illustration of consensus politics in *Dogville* (Lars von Trier, 2003) and *Mystic River* (Clint Eastwood, 2003), analysing both films in the context of the post-9/11 rhetoric of 'infinite justice'. Representative of the totalising rhetoric of Western governmental figures such as George W. Bush and Tony Blair, the construction of an absolute separation between good/evil, citizen/terrorist is played out in these films. What Rancière refers to as 'the contemporary ethical turn' refers to 'specific conjunction . . . between fact and law' which 'gives way to an unprecedented dramaturgy of infinite evil, justice and reparation' (Rancière 2010: 185). Both the 'ethical turn' and consensus refer to an increased allocation and reinforcement of circumscribed roles. This development in policy and rhetoric comes to inform Rancière's approach to the social violences staged in *Dogville* and *Mystic River*: 'the depoliticized national community, then, is set up just like the small community of *Dogville* – through the duplicity that at once fosters social services in the community and involves the absolute rejection of the other' (Rancière 2010: 189). The argument soon turns to debates on ethics in art – in particular, theories of 'the unrepresentable' by Theodor Adorno and Jean- François Lyotard. Just like the ethical turn in political discourse, unrepresentable art is said to produce 'an indistinction between right and fact' (ibid.: 195). Therefore, the ethical turn in politics and aesthetics installs a firm separation between the right and the wrong, stubbornly deflecting attempts to defy convention. By attaching firm moral frameworks, a rigid distribution of the sensible is realised, which in turn heightens defence against political interruption. By this point in the argument, the two filmic examples have already been left behind; they are used solely to illustrate the ethical turn's displacement of politics. *Dogville* is described as 'a transposition of a theatrical and political fable' (ibid.: 186). It is, in other words, no more than a useful illustration of consensus. This turn to cinema as a way of illustrating social configurations seems to contradict something more potent that Rancière locates in art generally. In *The Politics of Aesthetics* (2004), we are told that:

> The politics of works of art plays itself out to a larger extent . . . in the reconfiguration of worlds of experience based on which police consensus or political dissensus are defined . . . It is up to the various forms of politics to appropriate, for their own proper use, the modes of presentation or the means of establishing explanatory sequences produced by artistic practices rather than the other way around. (Rancière 2004: 65)

The political stakes of art in this text are far greater than those in later works on cinema. Politics should – and therefore, perceivably, could – follow aesthetic strategies initiated by works of art. Were we to take this perspective into a viewing of *Dogville*, we might ask far grander questions on the significance of the film's innovative style. For example, how might we understand the film's ascetic *mise en scène* as a challenge to the America it represents? Is there

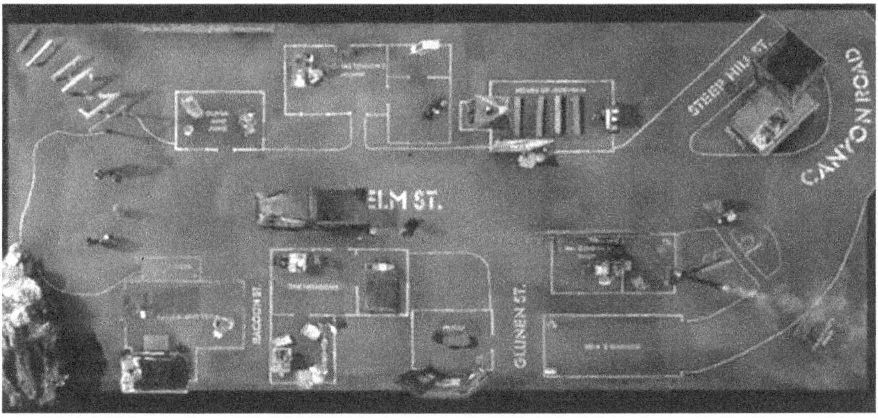

Figure I.2 The stripped-down *mise en scène* of *Dogville*.

a form of antagonism brought about through the social distribution made plain through the mapping of white lines on a black floor (Figure I.2)? These grander questions are the sort asked by Angelos Koutsourakis, who seeks to unpack 'the broader political implications of the film's experimental form' (2013: 147). Koutsourakis's analysis adopts what he calls a 'post-Brechtian' approach: a rejuvenated approach to political modernist theory that provides a critical yet affirmative vision of how cinema can be political. In so doing, Koutsourakis retains the radical tone of political modernism whilst remaining critical of some of its stultifying assumptions, offering hope for a politics of cinema beyond mere illustration. While I consistently side with Rancière in his critique of political modernism, it might yet be said that his dismissal of its methods might have come to obstruct his view of its primary intent. Like Koutsourakis, I too am concerned with exploring the broader social possibilities potentialised by cinema. Despite Rancière's continued neglect for cinema's political potential, such a hope exists, fleetingly, late in Rancière's essay: 'it would be easy to cite forms of political action and artistic intervention that are independent from, or hostile to, that dominant current' (2010: 201). While not present in 'The ethical turn of politics and aesthetics', I shall consider one final, recent analysis on the politics of cinema that engages with one such 'form'.

It is perhaps no surprise that a philosopher who has for so long prioritised the thoughts and actions of 'the poor' would be so interested in the films of Pedro Costa, who has produced what might be regarded as the most sustained engagement with the effects of globalisation and institutionally enforced poverty in the Western world. The urgency of Costa's films is addressed directly by Rancière himself, who claims that 'his central subject is also at the heart of contemporary politics – the fate of the exploited' (Rancière 2014b:

127). Unlike the circumscribing of Godard's films or the purely illustrative function of von Trier's, Costa's seem to provide a heightened political potential. This suggestion is made at first through the subject matter; but Rancière quickly argues that this is 'not sufficient' in itself:

> [A] mode of representation needs to be added, one which renders the situation intelligible as the effect of particular causes and shows it to generate forms of awareness and emotions that modify it . . . This is where things go wrong. Pedro Costa's camera never follows the normal trajectory of moving his lens away from the places of misery to the places where those in dominant positions producing this misery live. (ibid.: 127–8)

Costa's visual method is interesting for Rancière because the camera so often refuses to conform to earlier models of political aesthetics.[4] Solely concerned with the stories of the poor – not the systems of power beyond their immediate control – the political potential of Costa's approach derives from what Rancière describes as 'a people's art' (ibid.: 137). More than elsewhere in his writing on cinema, his analysis of *Colossal Youth* (2006) expresses a positive view of cinema's political potential. The film's protagonist, Ventura, is a Cape Verdean immigrant who has been relocated from the slums to a housing development on the outskirts of Lisbon. He has worked as a labourer, renovating the art gallery. Upon entering the gallery for leisure, he is accosted by the security guard, embodying the poor's displacement in a commune of the elite. This immediately invokes the failed dream for cinema imagined by Walter Benjamin: that of cinema's removal of the gallery's aura and its democratisation of the image for the masses (Benjamin 1968). Rancière argues that *Colossal Youth* offers an argument of this sort, through its comparison of the gallery and the slums. The gallery displays 'no obvious superiority'; the gilded frames of paintings appear to provide an 'even more trivial division of space than the window' of the slum (Rancière 2014b: 132). Echoing Benjamin while he implicitly critiques him, this gallery is described as: 'the place where art is shut inside a frame without transparency or reciprocity . . . that excludes the worker who built it' (ibid: 132–3). Rancière attaches to *Colossal Youth* a stronger conviction than his other writing on cinema, echoing the need signalled in *The Politics of Aesthetics* for politics to mobilise the work of art's 'reconfigurations of worlds of experience' (Rancière 2004: 65). Between the reality of Ventura (an amateur actor of Cape Verdean descent) and the diegesis, and between the narrative and the spectator's response to that narrative, worlds of experience are apparently reconfigured in *Colossal Youth*. As such, consensus is defined and undermined.

I take encouragement from Rancière's analysis of *Colossal Youth* that a politics of cinema may indeed exist. Yet, for all the benefits of thinking politics aesthetically and thinking cinema politically in the Rancièrian manner, there is in general an overriding sense of futility for films that desire more than merely 'politics in what a film is saying' or 'the specific strategy of an artistic approach' (Rancière 2014b: 104). I embrace Rancière's critique of political modernism's allegories of inequality, but I wish to challenge his assertion that there is no politics of cinema. Taking a more optimistic approach, I believe that the argument that films *only* talk about politics, or *only* aestheticise politics (in a Benjaminian manner),[5] is unnecessarily constrictive on what cinema might be. Even from a realist perspective, the argument is refutable: films *have* produced felt political change. I set out to show this with each chapter. From films that talk about politics (represent political history) to films that politicise the formal language (develop formal strategies that artistically construct and reconstruct distributions of the sensible), the *politique* of cinema carries with it a political potential that challenges Rancière's denial of a politics of cinema.

ART CINEMA

From the political modernist predilection for Godard to Rancière's own textual choices, it is fair to say that the same films considered political are often those also described as art cinema. But art cinema is an awkward term. On the one hand, it would seem to account for far too diverse a selection of styles to provide a determined statement. On the other hand, it has arisen quite organically as a way of accounting for a textual resistance to the mainstream. Since the term is used quite frequently in everyday and academic discourse, the vagueness of its meaning works ultimately to threaten its critical potential. Yet, a vast body of theoretical work exists that tries to demarcate a determined categorical status. Steve Neale broke ground in this sense when he departed from the commonplace assertions on *what* constitutes art cinema and began to analyse the effects of that constitution. He begins with the broadly accepted notion of art cinema as a counter-Hollywood stylistic mode, arguing that to oppose classical Hollywood style is to oppose the masking of societal tensions (Neale 1981: 14). Neale's ultimate aim is to unpack the cultural economy of art cinema. For all their stylistic complexity and in spite of their resistance to the globally dominant mode, for Neale, art cinema is merely a bourgeois category, marked by its 'basis in commodity-dominated modes of production, distribution and exhibition, and by the repetitions that tend to mark cultural discourses in general and the discourses of high art and culture in particular' (ibid.: 15). Neale's negative view of art cinema is reminiscent of Theodor Adorno and Max Horkheimer's cynical view of the film industry in general. Wholly damning of cinema's capacity to become a democratic medium in the service of the people, cinema is no more than a 'culture industry', adept at reproducing marketable produce. Referring to one particularly notable art film practitioner, Adorno and Horkheimer insist that subversions against the norm merely serve to reinforce the power of the industry:

> Whenever Orson Welles offends against the tricks of the trade, he is forgiven because his departures from the norm are regarded as calculated mutations which serve all the more strongly to confirm the validity of the system. The constraint of the technically-conditioned idiom which stars and directors have to produce as 'nature' so that the people can appropriate it, extends to such fine nuances that they almost attain the subtlety of the devices of an avant-garde work as against those of truth. (Adorno and Horkheimer 1997: 129)

As shown here, the argument that art films are no less subservient to the profit motive than mainstream fare clearly has a history in cultural theory. This Frankfurt School mode of cultural criticism remains popular and vital to theories of political aesthetics. However, just like any totalising theory, the attempt to deny altogether any critical potential arising within such a broad category needs to be challenged. I wish to respond to this approach in two ways – briefly, for now, but in detail throughout each of my chapters. The first concerns the place where political activity might be located. The second more directly contests the notion of art cinema as an inherently bourgeois institution that sustains an exploitative division of labour (Neale 1981: 36).

Art cinema can be viewed to offer a political potential if we reconsider the category outside of broad sociological terms and consider instead the specific innovations occurring on the textual level. For instance, while Neale is quick to dismiss the humanistic impulse of Italian neorealism – which he describes as 'the very paradigm of Art Cinema' (1981: 26) – the continued stylistic influence of neorealism can be traced throughout late twentieth- and early twenty-first-century cinematic movements, in places as far reaching as Chile, to Iran, to Romania. That its influence is felt in the most socially engaged cinematic new waves challenges the straightforward dismissal of art film stylistic sensibilities. Such a resonance with social antagonism and revelation is, it appears, emblematic of art cinema's ability to broach what Andre Bazin described as 'the continuum of reality' (Bazin 1967: 37); or, in Gilles Deleuze's terms, to repeat the historical 'break' from classical narrative movement (Deleuze 1985: x). In these terms, art films of today are similarly concerned with balancing the incisive vision of the documentarist with the creative experimentation of the avant-garde artist.

In other terms, the category of art cinema is far too stylistically disparate to dismiss its motivations as cleanly as Neale suggests. He even implies this through his overview of art film auteurs, showing that variety is symptomatic of each art film's distinct opposition to Hollywood. However, as Thomas Elsaesser has argued, 'viewing the Hollywood/Europe divide as merely the special case of a more general process of generic differentiation, where films are valued, canonized, or have re-assigned to them identities and meanings according to often apparently superficial or secondary characteristics, can be very instructive indeed' (Elsaesser 2005: 45–6). As Elsaesser suggests, the ground for setting up a straightforward binary between art cinema and Hollywood is shaky. Taking the opposite route to Elsaesser, we may even dispute the idea that art cinema is essentially in conversation with Hollywood at all. Either way, Neale's dichotomising of art and entertainment discounts a great many alternative reasons for the stylistic particularity of each art film. Alternative categories may include national or cultural specificity; art historical lineage; conceptuality; subverting within genre; or technological experimentation. These are just a few of the diverse motivations informing the distinct stylistic decisions of art filmmakers that need not imply a conversation with Hollywood cinema. A more effective approach, I think, would be to historicise the differences and similarities throughout the myriad stylistic and thematic motivations of art filmmakers. James Tweedie has argued along these lines, demonstrating how the development of art cinema in post-war Europe can be viewed as part and parcel of a seismic, cultural shift towards the global:

> The art cinema of the 1950s and after has drifted constantly between high and low traditions, between popular media and rarefied art, between transnational youth culture and the gallery or museum; it is 'culture' in the elevated and universalized, the archaic and contemporary, senses of the word. What the cinematic new waves have globalized is a hybrid, mutually contaminated cultural category – art cinema – that lies at the border of mass communication and art. (Tweedie 2013: 3)

Tweedie's attachment of new waves occurring in Western Europe shortly before its spread throughout Eastern Europe, Africa, Asia and Latin America shows how, globally, art cinema has been the mode of choice for films that combine technical innovation with critical social commentary. Tweedie's approach allows us to formulate a subtler sociological understanding of art cinema than Neale's. But this geopolitical engagement is just one way of determining the political potential of art cinema. Such approaches tend often to order the textual properties around a sociological illustration in ways not dissimilar to Rancière's view of cinema as theoretical transposition. This is particularly apparent when a filmmaker like Věra Chytilová is read in dialogue with the revolution in Czechoslovakia in the late 1960s (Tweedie 2013: 33). How can one account for the stylistic audacity and anarchic tone of a film like

Daisies (1966) wholly within the context of organised dissent and global youth culture? While more positive and culturally sensitive than Neale's analysis, such an analytical frame remains prohibitive. If we are to move beyond the political modernist trait of stultification, a mode of analysis is needed that recognises the spectator's autonomy and the reality of subjective universality across the cinema audience. To this extent, a more appropriate feature on which to focus would be the heterogeneous quality of the art cinema. Rosalind Galt and Karl Schoonover locate heterogeneity throughout the industry of art film as well as in the texts themselves. Galt and Schoonover have determined a five-point schema for determining what constitutes art cinema: (1) a film's traversing of mainstream and alternative spaces of exhibition; (2) international marketability; (3) its ambivalent relationship with industrial categories (like stardom); (4) its troubling of genre categories; and (5) its recognition of diverse spectatorship through a dual register of anti-specular intellectualism and pro-specular affectivity (Galt and Schoonover 2010: 7–8). While it would be foolish to ally films that tick these boxes with politics outright, such a broad schema provides a comprehensive way of accounting for the heterogeneity of style, production, forms and modes of reception these films invoke. Galt and Schoonover's art film 'brings categories into question and holds the potential to open up spaces between and outside of mainstream/avant-garde, local/cosmopolitan, history/theory, and industrial/formal debates in film scholarship' (ibid.: 9). To explain how this characteristic heterogeneity informs a political aesthetic, I would like to draw an analogy between Galt and Schoonover's definition of art cinema and what Rancière describes as 'the aesthetic regime of art': a regime that 'strictly identifies art in the singular and frees it from any specific rule, from any hierarchy in the arts, subject matter and genres' (2004: 18).

The aesthetic regime of art is the third historical category in Rancière's discussion of political aesthetics. It breaks from both the initial 'ethical regime of images' (whereby art is approached solely for its social worth) and the 'poetic/representative regime of the arts' (which accounts for the performative relevance of art, according to mimetic artistic categories). Defined according to the Romantic philosophies of Kant and Schiller, the break occurs when the demarcation that separates proper forms and purposes from the undefined, is dissolved. Artistic form is subsequently experienced for itself (Rancière 2004: 24). In this way, the aesthetic regime is marked by a self-awareness that comes to foreground the process, or constructedness, of artistry itself. Galt and Schoonover note an identical convention across art films, defining such awareness as emblematic of twentieth-century art in general (2010: 19). This echoes the argumentation of Clement Greenberg, who defined modernist art through a 'self-criticism' that is performed 'from the inside, through the procedures themselves of that which is criticized' (Greenberg 1990: 94).

Greenberg maintains that the removal of depth in the artwork abandons 'the representation of recognizable objects in principle' (Greenberg 1990: 96), thus revealing the most essential components of the medium. Rancière's aesthetic regime shares much with Greenberg's formally self-critical art. However, unlike Greenberg, he challenges the teleological take on 'modernity's destiny' (2004: 25). Embodied by Greenberg's famous essay, such a tendency to brand a 'distinctive feature of art' (ibid.: 28) is repeated, he claims, throughout post-modern theories of art. In its place, the aesthetic regime is attendant to a fluidity between artistic regimes. Distinctions between, and hierarchies amongst, *the arts*, are levelled. In their place, a discourse on a singular *art* is erected in its place. A category founded in the spirit of antagonising categories, then, the heterogeneity of art films is clearest when the borders between the arts are tested in the spirit of redefining cinema itself. In other words, as a cinema of the formally interruptive (*art*), rather than the categorical, bourgeois and abrasively cerebral (*the arts*), art cinema emblematises the heterogeneity essential to the aesthetic regime. As shown in each of my analyses, this gesture is one of the defining features of contemporary political art cinema.

This summary defines art cinema through heterogeneity on industrial, stylistic, thematic and affective levels. Turning to Rancière's attention to the politics of aesthetics, the political potential of art cinema arises out of the stylistic and technological fluidity that defines the aesthetic regime of art. The political quality of this emanates, in Gabriel Rockhill's terms, through 'promoting the equality of represented subjects, the indifference of style with regard to content, and the immanence of meaning in things themselves' (Rockhill 2004: 81). While Neale argued towards the institutionalising effects of the cultural economy of art cinema, then, that it can equally be defined as heterogeneous on so many levels surely undoes the totality of those claims. Art films are frequently engaged in unsettling cinematic distributions of the sensible in ways constitutive of what Rancière described as 'political art' (Rancière 2004: 63).

My second dispute with the Frankfurt School approach of Neale regards the branding of all art cinema as conservative: 'a mechanism of discrimination . . . a means of producing and sustaining a division within the field of cinema overall, a division that functions economically, ideologically and aesthetically' (Neale 1981: 37). Irrespective of the political potential that exists on a textual level, the reality of art film reception is quite different. Indeed, arthouse cinemas, whilst far more likely to be screening socially committed films, are also far more likely to host people of economic privilege than the contemporary multiplex. Barbara Willinsky's study of arthouse history in the US, *Sure Seaters: The Emergence of Arthouse Cinema* (2001), explains how the emergence of the arthouse in the US provided a haven for the development of middle-brow culture and an affordable site of leisure for the burgeoning middle class at a time of social and economic change. For Willinsky, arthouse cinemas 'offered spaces that encouraged audience members to think and talk about the films in an intellectual manner' (Willinsky 2001: 89). There are two problems with this perspective. The first regards the commonplace critical binary between active and passive spectatorship discussed previously. While the arthouse provides a space for middlebrow culture, this does not negate the strong probability that cognitive activity had been occurring in nickelodeons, movie palaces and popular cinemas at the time. Neither does the arthouse's existence discount the capacity for the spectators in multiplex cinemas of the twenty first century to view and think critically. The second issue is one that allows us to make headway towards defining the politics of art cinema. While I accept that art films are often made with the expectation of a bourgeois audience, this is not to say that these films cater for such an audience. There is no strictly determined schema for distinguishing between bourgeois art films and anti-bourgeois art films. As such – and prompted by this dispute with Neale and Willinsky – I am keen to ask one clear question in each my analyses: *to whom do these films speak?* The answer to this question will allow us to determine the social ethos and political potential of any art film.

The selection of films throughout demonstrates, I think, that politically fertile art films distinguish themselves from Neale's institutionalised art cinema when they address an *us*, a *we*, a *people*. These films hold this potential when they do so not with the intention of exclusively reinforcing the *us* that already exists, but of insisting upon its expansion. The films I discuss are engaged in inviting political action, in the vein of what Nico Baumbach termed an 'aesthetic model' (Baumbach 2013: 28). By mobilising 'art' in the Rancièrian sense, I wish to claim that the democratic spirit of the aesthetic regime is most apparent in this kind of cinema.

A CINEMA OF POLITICS AND A POLITICS OF CINEMA

I have divided my analyses into three sections. The first two sections are an attempt to maintain the paradoxes of Rancière's idea for a 'political art' that situates itself between 'the readability of the message that threatens to destroy the sensible form of art and the radical uncanniness that threatens to destroy all *political* meaning' (author's italics; Rancière 2004: 63). By simultaneously referring to politics as both an aesthetic activity and the more commonplace definition of 'politics' (of nations, governments, social movements), Rancière raises an enlightening contradiction. It is for this reason that I distinguish between a 'cinema of politics' (films that signify 'politics') and a 'politics of cinema' (films that perform politics in spite of their lack of 'political' signification). The cinema of politics makes subtle gestures to a history of 'political cinema' but also the possibility of a Rancièrian politics occurring within these representational texts. This section engages with cinema's attempts to directly represent what is normally perceived as 'politics': the activities of state mechanisms, their structures of power and their effects on citizens. My first chapter explores the notion of 'disagreement' in Jafar Panahi's seminal video-diary, *This is Not a Film* (2011). Panahi's story is relatively well known. A persecuted artist in a theocratic state, he has been banned from making films and placed under house arrest after having been found guilty of producing agitational films. Despite its apparently negative title, Panahi's 'non-film' presents an aesthetic politics: it is an attempt by the voiceless to voice himself, antagonising with the police order that restricts him to a specific space and prevents him from moving outside of it. His challenge to what is and is not film presents a challenge to the ontological foundations governing cinema, intrinsically realigning the partitions between what counts as a film and what does not.

The second chapter moves from discussion of Middle Eastern political prisoners to a historical narrative that is underrepresented in Western news coverage: the dictatorship of Augusto Pinochet in Chile. A pivotal point in the development of global neoliberalism, Pinochet's dictatorship through the 1970s and 1980s came to an end after diplomatic pressure from overseas resulted in the holding of a plebiscite to decide on his continued reign. Pablo Larraín (the son of a conservative supporter of the dictatorship) is the first filmmaker to engage directly with the coup (in *Post Mortem* [2010]) and the movement to democracy (in *No* [2012]). Since these films do not offer conventionally polemical portrayals of the atrocities committed, many Latin American commentators have dismissed the films as simplistic, even apologetic of the crimes committed. Proposing an alternative position, I shall argue that Larraín attempts to resuscitate this historical narrative with a peculiar form of aesthetic politics. Incorporating discussion of the political ambivalence that Rancière prioritises in the discipline of historiography (Rancière 1994), I shall claim that *No*'s non-partisan representation of the events surrounding the end of dictatorship returns us to a political past to make profound observations on the present. Drawing attention to the film's self-reflexive characterisation and its use of time-specific technologies, I argue that Larraín's approach utilises ambivalent techniques to assume a position of immanent critique.

The third and fourth chapters offer accounts of what I call 'a politics of cinema': avowedly non-political films that potentialise politics through cinematic form and the social relationships constructed with their spectators. The first of these is Charlie Kaufman's *Synecdoche, New York* (2008). Kaufman's film (about a man losing his mind and seeking catharsis through the production of a play that involves the theatrically staged replication of New York City) confronts the postmodern claim that we live in a time after politics, devoid of difference, insistent on consensus. The film's coupling of sardonic cultural critique and formal play produces a novel perspective that pronounces the possibility of difference within and against consensus. In making this claim, I counter a dominant perception in existing scholarship that views the film as an elaboration of Jean Baudrillard's critical commentaries on Western simulated realities. Not simply representing the annulment of individuality and political engagement in contemporary America, I argue towards a consideration of the film as an example of what Rancière calls 'dissensus': the heterogeneous 'presence of two worlds in one' (Rancière 2010: 69).

Chapter 4 turns to the avowedly unpolitical cinema of Nuri Bilge Ceylan.[6] A twenty-first-century humanist, comparable to the likes of Yasujiro Ozu, Ingmar Bergman or Andrey Tarkovsky, Ceylan seems more interested in the existential dilemmas surrounding the difficulties of social relationships than in the overcoming of inequalities. However, in *Climates* (2006), Ceylan's drawing upon extra-cinematic, autobiographical elements raises some significant ideas about the relationship between an author and a spectator. After the postmodern 'death of the author' (Barthes 1977), Ceylan's traversing of roles (as director, star and, I claim, the person upon whom the film is clearly based) reasserts the importance of the author figure not as a form of nostalgic longing but as a gesture towards the dismantling of the hierarchy that exists in cinematic spectatorship. Ceylan's equality does not stem from the attempts to revolutionise art by removing the artist; instead it occurs through a redistribution of the roles involved in the participatory experience of cinema. Further inferred through the film's formal elements, equality is a presupposition that results in the political partitioning of sensible orders (such as the film's fragmentary images, editing style and the partition between dreams and reality).

Chapter 5 turns to a film that troubles the neat divide I have constructed thus far, posing the question: how might we envision a film whose signification is no more political than it is artistic? If there is a space for the paradoxical function of 'political art', might we undermine the conscious divide I insert between them? The work of John Akomfrah presents a convincing case. In Akomfrah's essay film *The Nine Muses* (2010) the aesthetic paradigms of politics and art are broached so evenly that it is as possible to speak of a 'cinema of politics' as it is to speak of a 'politics of cinema' – both concepts are equalised, so that each is constitutive of the other. A bricolage of extraordinary intertextuality, Akomfrah's film is equally concerned with the socio-historical problem of migrant subjectivity and the politico-aesthetic distribution of hierarchies relating to forms and technologies of art. The thematic concern for migration becomes a formal 'foreignness', creating a reconfigurative possibility for cinema and its adjacent art forms. Following Rancière's utopian framing of the 'foreigner' (2003: 3), I shall claim that *The Nine Muses* utilises this conceptual figure who 'persists in the curiosity of his gaze, displaces his angle of vision, reworks the first way of putting together words and images, undoes the certainties of place' (ibid.: 3). I wish to argue that the foreigner is an urgent political concept at a time of consensus and especially crucial in regards to public responses to the present-day refugee crisis. Always inferring something beyond the stable, police order, always challenging the homogeneity of reality in its apparent state, the foreigner speaks for more than the migrant people of Akomfrah's film. It is a symbol that in spite of enduring voicelessness, the disparity of apparent political subjectivity in the world is at odds with our history, our art, our culture. Working across exhibition platforms, Akomfrah's practice signals a foreign aesthetic and offers, with *The Nine Muses*, profound insight into the political potential of cinema.

NOTES

1. Todd May's *The Political Thought of Jacques Rancière* (2008) and Samuel A. Chambers' *The Lessons of Rancière* (2013) are particularly significant in this regard.
2. And while his key text of political philosophy, *Disagreement*, opens with the provocative question 'is there any such thing as political philosophy?' (Rancière 1999: vii), the dialogues he subsequently opens onto with the classics, the ancients, idealists and twentieth-century political thought, represent a persistent concern for, and discursive encounter with, philosophy proper.
3. D. N. Rodowick's *The Crisis of Political Modernism* (1994) takes Harvey's term as its starting point in order to review the what he described as its 'inevitable impasse' (1994: 6). Rodowick's argument – like many of the early 1990s – is informed by the contemporary intellectual environment's dissatisfaction with totalising political theories. Political modernism was ultimately doomed due to its hostile dogmatism. Later, in *The Politics of Hollywood Cinema* (2013), Richard Rushton revisits these debates and takes up the arguments of a number of contemporary political philosophers (including Rancière) in order to demonstrate the close binds of cinema and democracy.
4. The primary reference points are political modernist in style – the alienation practised by Straub and Huillet is mentioned. However, he also mentions Francesco Rosi (Rancière 2014b: 128), whose poetic brand of social realism can be located in political cinematic history instigated by the neorealists and joined by later socially conscious filmmakers such as Ken Loach and the Dardennes.
5. This idea of political strategy through the formal qualities of a text was most memorably expressed through Walter Benjamin's conclusion in 'The work of art in the age of mechanical reproduction' (1968), whereby communist art is seen to perform an 'aestheticisation of politics'.
6. In an interview recorded for the Artifical Eye DVD release of *Climates*, Ceylan addresses attempts by some journalists to frame his films in a political context, urging people not to view his films as political.

PART I

A Cinema of Politics

CHAPTER 1

Panahi's Disagreement

> Disagreement occurs wherever contention over what speaking means constitutes the very rationality of the speech situation . . . It is less concerned with arguing than with what can be argued, the presence or absence of a common object between X and Y. It concerns the tangible presentation of this common object, the very capacity of the interlocutors to present it.
>
> (Rancière 1999: xi–xii)

Disagreement carries a dual meaning, encompassing both the point being disputed and the terms used to define that dispute. Jafar Panahi's *This is Not a Film* (2011) provides a major example of disagreement in cinema from recent years. It concerns the depiction of a real life through the generically familiar, documentary tradition of political cinema. It takes as its subject matter a dispute with the Iranian government, channelling the relationship between dissent, conspiracy and activism that we find throughout the political cinema tradition (from Eisenstein through Gillo Pontecorvo, Costa-Gavras and Oliver Stone). In 2010, Panahi was banned from making and exhibiting films. His house imprisonment (as documented in *This is Not a Film*) was a temporary measure while awaiting trial for his crimes. However, the peculiar thing about *This is Not a Film* is Panahi's self-conscious determination to avoid matters of the social, making this this film stranger than it might first appear.

Closer insight into the events that occur in the film demonstrate Panahi's determination to avoid this topic. Rather than framing what follows in the 'expository mode' of documentary – the primary means of relaying information and persuasively making a case since at least the 1920s (Nichols 1991: 34) – *This is Not a Film* is more a deliberation on how one passes the time spent in incarceration. We mostly watch Panahi discussing – with collaborator and camera operator Mojtaba Mirtahmasb – the production of a film he was banned from making; performing mundane domestic chores; talking with friends and family; quietly, pensively waiting. This is an insight into a particular experience of censorship, over and above inquiry into the cultural circumstances of how censorship occurs. Yet, by documenting this avoidance on camera, he nonetheless has made a *film*. Extending debates framed in my introduction, I wish to argue that the political significance of Panahi's film derives not from the state context surrounding its production – it occurs instead through the aesthetic parameters negotiated by Panahi in the space of the film itself. This negotiation is constitutive of a political redistribution of the sensible. *This is Not a Film* embodies the dual process of disagreement by dissenting against both his sentence and the terms used to define that sentence. Panahi's initial disagreement – the claim that 'this is not a film' – reverberates through a number of subsequent formal disagreements, redistributing the sensible arrangements of Panahi's confined social situation. As such, Panahi's disagreement is not a form of negation; rather, it exhibits a political subjectification demonstrative of his 'capacity for enunciation' (Rancière 1999: 36).

As I explained in the introduction, political subjectification in the Rancièrian sense departs from what Althusser called 'state apparatus' and what Foucault called 'power'. Althusser's 'state apparatuses' are bodies of control, governing the organisation of society, ensuring the continuing domination of the many by the ruling classes (Althusser 1971). Here, then, politics is an activity that is apparently predetermined by the known doctrines of Marxist political theory. While not generally affiliated with Marxist theory, Foucault mirrors Althusser in his equation of politics with the organisation of power. When he discusses Jeremy Bentham's panopticon as a metaphor for society (1975) or 'biopolitics' (2008), political activity is shown to be an act of oppression, functioning to *subject* people to particular roles in society rather than *subjectifying* the people through their capacity to realise and undertake new, non-prescribed roles. Politics as disagreement is a marked departure from both concepts. Not simply acknowledgment of the power exerted through social structures, politics here refers solely to events that demonstrate a perceivable antagonism with these police structures: 'nothing is political in itself merely because power relations are at work in it. For a thing to be political, it must give rise to a meeting of police logic and egalitarian logic that is never set up in advance' (Rancière 2010: 32). Rancière's definition breaks from the equation of politics with existing power structures. Instead, it realigns political activity with antagonisms performed *in conflict with* those structures. Political events are, therefore, defined by (1) a disagreement with a police's enforcement of power, which is in turn (2) a disagreement with that police's tangible configuration of the social order into groups of inclusion and exclusion. Politics concerns solely the encroachment by a person into a social distribution from which they were previously excluded. As we see in *This is Not a Film*, Panahi's disagreement is the result of attempts to intervene in the order of things. His response (meagre though he often bemoans it) builds towards the rearrangement of the aesthetic distribution enforced by the Iranian state. Disagreement is never set up in advance: it arises as a specific response to a particular police order.

Panahi's meagre attempts are referred to in the film as 'efforts'. Efforts are needed to instigate the process of going from 'a part of those who have no part' to a political agent. As I shall explain through my analysis, *This is Not a Film* stages the clash between Panahi's 'egalitarian logic' and the Iranian 'police logic', constituting what I term an *aesthetics of effort*. The necessary effort arrived at in *This is Not a Film* appears in the epiphany, 'keep the camera on', resulting subsequently in the filming of everything and the recurring long takes that result. Panahi's aesthetics of effort come to inform a way of doing cinema, both compounding and alluding to the contradiction of the film's title: a film that is 'not a film'. While this is just a man sitting around in an apartment and, therefore, 'not a film', this opens out onto the possibility of politics: redistributing the sensible dimensions of the point being disputed and the terms used to define that dispute (Panahi's imprisonment and the cinematic medium). As I shall come to explain, Panahi's is a peculiar form of cinema that evolves before our eyes in the film itself, altering the ontological frames that determine what is and is not film and what is and is not politics.

I turn first to the early scenes, where Panahi outlines the many prohibitions his incarceration entails. These scenes illustrate the 'message' (Rancière 2004: 63) approach by stressing a preferred meaning, in turn destroying both the sensible form of art and its potential for political dialogue with the spectator. *This is Not a Film* hereby stages the stultifying effects of images that either too overtly or symbolically refer to the social problem of censorship and political imprisonment. These scenes provide a useful counterpoint to the film's aesthetics of effort and a pertinent place to ask the question, *what is it about this film that is not a film?*

POLICING THE FILMIC

Rancière states that 'political art' should contain a message, but that this message should be threatened by something beyond the terms of its signification – something he calls 'uncanny', alluding to the involvement of the spectator (Rancière 2004: 63). This point is more clearly developed in *The Emancipated Spectator* (2009c), when he decries the alienating Brechtianisms of some artists and the immersive Artaudianisms of others. His point is that spectators will always engage with a performance, but only ever on their own, cognate, terms. This uncanny double effect acknowledges the spectator's participation and with it a paradoxical clash: between the spectator's judgement and the apparent import of the text itself. *This is Not a Film* embraces the emancipatory uncanniness of spectatorship, but it also illustrates precisely the overly didactic tendencies of its Brechtian predecessors. Usually this avoidance of didacticism is to Panahi's credit, but sometimes it is harder to say. This first point will discuss moments in which the former (which are akin to what Rancière describes as 'political art') outweigh the latter moments (which attempt to contain the engagement of a film spectator within the space of the text's more overt levels of meaning). The most noteworthy scenes in this regard are the moments involving discussion of his case.

Panahi is pictured sitting at his kitchen table using a speakerphone; both voices are heard. At the outset of the film, then again later, legal advisors relay his reasonable chances of a reduced sentence, but his slim chance that the charges will be dropped altogether. These scenes mainly serve the purpose of describing facts and, in that sense, this is as close as the film comes to the more conventional mode of the orthodox current affairs, political documentary. One is reminded of the performative style of Michael Moore, when he learns of people's fates and confronts villains in activist documentaries such as *Fahrenheit 9/11* (2004). More pertinent than the content of the information is his expressive response to hearing the facts. The camera's focus on his response to learning his fate situates the film in the generic location of investigative documentary: character-led stories showing a person's struggle through a trying situation. These scenes break little new aesthetic ground, beyond the revelation of Panahi's own story; they solely present the readability of a message. The other main scenes that are concerned primarily with the presentation of a message are Panahi's filmic analyses. On two occasions, in order to articulate his feelings about the situation, he plays scenes from his films to the camera. One occurs in the first ten minutes, when he shows us a scene from *The Mirror* (1997). A young girl (Mena, the film's protagonist) gets sick of performing and decides to walk off set. Panahi uses this moment to describe his own situation: like Mena, he tells us, he 'throws away the cast' by talking directly to the camera. This direct address to the spectator allows him to express himself more clearly, ensuring no confusion as to his thought process. This is a marked change from his well-known preference for amateur performance, banal events and the contingency of narrative and poetic realist aesthetics, which some have described as 'Iranian neorealism' (Dabashi 2001; Chaudhuri and Finn 2003; Weinberger 2007; Giovacchini and Sklar 2012). Denying the poetic subtleties available to cinematic fiction, Panahi seeks solely to explain things in a clear manner. Immediately, then, Panahi has attempted to remove the dialogical set-up of the Rancièrian political art. His revisiting of old films turns this into a 'message film': its primary aim is the clear transference of a particular point. The conveyance of a message in the form of direct address is the formal reason for Panahi's defining this as 'non-film'. However, rather than dismissing these sections as didactic shortfalls, they serve rather as the vital counterpoint of the political art film. He clarifies this in the second analysis scene, when Mirtahmasb refers to what they are doing as 'a film' and he cynically replies, 'you call this a film?!' His later analyses are an even stronger portrayal of the counter-cinematic act of direct address.

Even more than with his analysis of *The Mirror*, Panahi demonstrates the non-filmic analyses of other films by applying an extended commentary in later scenes. He plays clips from *The Circle* (2000) and *Crimson Gold* (2003) in order to demonstrate how his earlier films show us cinema's ability to depict something unforeseen. These are fascinating insights, providing the most ardent cinephile with richly inventive detail on the poetic capacity of everyday life. For Panahi, like the neorealists before him, contingency and beauty in everyday life are essential features of cinema. These qualities define the very nature of cinema and, in turn, define that which lacks such qualities as non-filmic. The performance of the protagonist in *Crimson Gold* and the *mise en scène* that dwarfs the protagonist in *The Circle* are both examples of this. Purposefully intervening here through the act of explanation, Panahi insists that *This is Not a Film* cannot possibly achieve the same feat. Such moments of analysis, fascinating though they are, serve to demonstrate the limitations of Panahi's situation: confined to the space of his home with scant resources, he is forced to make something he himself would never refer to as a film and, because of its didacticism, Rancière would not refer to as politics.

At a time when it seems everything has been filmed and nothing escapes the field of vision, these scenes of filmic analysis can be viewed as an attempt to identify what we can distinguish from cinema and declare *not a film*. Furthermore, since, in Rancière's terms, the message obliterates the possibility of radical uncanniness, these scenes are also not constitutive of political art. Further still, in the terms of disagreement, since these scenes involve only a formal illustration of what is film (the ability for the earlier films to capture something contingent) and what is not (his current predicament, which has so cruelly removed this possibility), they cannot be described as politics in Rancière's terms. Their interest in the allocation of roles and distinction between film and non-film is more fitting to the definition of what Rancière calls 'police'. Panahi uses these moments to *police the filmic*, cynically and depressively segregating it from his present scenario.

The policing of the filmic also occurs in a subtler way through the image alone. There are moments when the *mise en scène* functions in a more overtly symbolic way. Even though these images are symbolic and, therefore, do not signify their purpose explicitly, the symbolism invoked is far from the 'radical uncanniness that threatens political meaning' (Rancière 2004: 63). The most transparent of these images occurs when Panahi stands on his balcony, looking at the world outside. We are placed behind him as he watches the construction of a new apartment block before him. We cannot know his expression or what he is thinking. This enigmatic image is forestalled, however, when the crane we have viewed in operation outside turns itself towards Panahi's apartment. We view it just long enough to enter the frame and depart again, before cutting to a new scene. Could this be a symbolic representation for the enormity of the state's surveillance programme – the inescapability of the state police? The crane, looming over Panahi as he tries to look out onto the world, is a stark reminder of the 'long arm of the law'. Holding the stationary camera on this estranging metonymy, the crane serves as a brazenly metaphorical indication of what is not a film for Panahi and what is not political art for Rancière.

There are other moments that invite a more symbolic reading. For instance, in the early scenes, when Panahi discusses *The Mirror*, the DVDs on the shelf above the television are all anonymously cased in black, apart from one oddity: the Hollywood thriller *Buried* (Rodrigo Cortes, 2010). Even without subscribing to a hierarchy of taste that precludes the association of Panahi with Hollywood, the appearance of this film in the image is jarring. *Buried* tells the story of an American truck driver who is taken hostage in Iraq and imprisoned below ground in a coffin. Setting aside the more obvious geopolitical implications of its narrative, the title and synopsis alone indicates a straightforward association with Panahi's situation: an innocent bystander is imprisoned in the Middle East as the result of state policing measures.

We might also interpret the persistent interest in Panahi's pet iguana, Igi, as a symbolic figure. In one scene, when Panahi is using his laptop for research, Igi crawls atop him and prevents him from typing. Is this iguana not just the kind of creature one would use to personify an oppressive state apparatus? The reptile has the appearance of a stereotypical, 'bad guy' figure; but there is something else here, too, which unsettles the straightforward connection of Igi to surveillant officer. While this creepy reptile plays the role well, the camera's strangely persistent returning to the creature thwarts the simplicity of this message. We sometimes see Igi wandering around the apartment with no discernible meaning behind the image whatsoever. This device is even used to counter the most readable of scenes. During one of Panahi's phone calls about the case, the camera pans away to trace Igi's movements as he climbs the bookcase (Figure 1.1). While we hear the conversation in the background, the symbolic dimension of Igi crawling amongst the books is less immediately decipherable than his earlier disruption to Panahi's work. In fact, so jarring is Igi's presence in this moment, it works to distract from the conversation in the background altogether. In other words, as much as the film invites us to read the creature as a symbol, it also offers Igi as a surreal deviation from the political signification: it is a moment of radical uncanniness that threatens the intelligibility of the message. While prior symbols and dialogues function to

Figure 1.1 *This is Not a Film*: Igi draws the spectator's attention away, visually interrupting the important phone conversation.

express a clear point to the spectator, Igi is a challenge to our comprehension and, as such, constitutes a moment of disagreement.

Such moments of disagreement are common in *This is Not a Film*. In fact, it is fair to say that the film itself is truer to the spirit of undermining political signification than it is of portraying it. Therefore, while it is important to recognise the film's persistent return to the limitations of its context, it also takes great strides in the opposite direction, challenging the physical and aesthetic policing imposed on Panahi. These strides – from here referred to as *efforts* – are truer to the poetic style of Panahi's earlier films and demonstrative of the radical uncanniness constitutive of political art. In my second point, I shall elaborate on the way effort shows itself, extending the process of disagreement as a form of politics towards a distinct form of art cinema. Panahi's efforts are wilful disagreements with the police order: disputing both the law and the terms used to create that law.

AN AESTHETICS OF EFFORT

Effort is uttered in *This is Not a Film* on a number of occasions. It refers to the need to try, with whatever meagre means at one's disposal, to oppose the system. It is first mentioned in the film's opening sequence, as we watch Panahi eating breakfast in front of the camera as he speaks to his colleague (whom we will learn is Mirtahmasb) on the phone. The colleague tells Panahi that he is in the process of 'making an effort' to produce a new documentary. Soon after, Panahi is shown in another telephone conversation, this time with a legal adviser. She tells him, in order to make some headway in his appeal, 'efforts' will be necessary in the filmmaking community. Later, as Mirtahmasb leaves the apartment, he advises Panahi to 'make an effort' to record everything. Each time we hear this, Panahi's face fills the frame, pronouncing the fact that it is he who is being advised to 'make an effort'. Thus, to have any chance of overcoming his sentence, Panahi must exert his own wilful effort. In this second point, I shall align effort with the philosophical concept of *will*. Disagreement – in this case, contention over what it means to make a film – is shown to be heavily reliant on the will of Panahi. In demonstrating his effort to challenge the terms of his confinement, Panahi presents the centrality of will to a Rancièrian politics. This is not to say that Panahi can simply *will himself out of* the situation; but, as an anti-representational mode of politics, it is a necessary component. To explain the nuances of this distinction and the extent to which will pre-empts politics, I shall attempt to distinguish between Rancière's disagreement and some classical political philosophies of will.

Will refers to the inclination to act on individual desires. These are routinely contrary to what is immediately at one's disposal. We often hear of 'the will to change' and the political weight of this saying is clear. The great philosophers of equality, whose influence on Rancière is easy to detect, have all discussed will at some stage. For Jean-Jacques Rousseau, a 'social contract' was required to manage the particular will of individuals, which would inevitably come into dispute with what he termed the 'general will' (Rousseau [1762] 2008). For Rousseau, society could only function if these particular wills could be negotiated in some way, within, by and for the state. As Joshua Cohen explains, 'the social bond is not simply the sum of private interests: those interests are in some ways opposed, and it is, again, their opposition that makes authoritative social coordination necessary' (Cohen 2010: 39). Cohen finds in Rousseau a guiding concern for equality amongst people *within* a state police through 'the common interest which unites them' (Rousseau 2008: 17). It is important for Rousseau that this social bond arises organically, within a small locality, rather than with force from above. As Roger D. Masters explains, on *The Social Contract*, 'the larger the State, the less likely that the political institutions will truly reflect the sovereign general will' (Masters 1968: 393). It is fair, then, to surmise that Rancière takes from Rousseau this view of individuals' shared capacity to act according to one's own will and determination.

While Rousseau's general will involves an organic form of sociality removed from strict formal governance, G. W. F. Hegel argues that, for society to function, a firm state police is a necessary measure. In *Outlines of the Philosophy of Right* ([1820] 2008), Hegel counters Rousseau's ideas on private will and individual liberties, explaining how such freedoms amounted to the kind of terror executed in the name of Jacobinism during the French revolution. Taken to extreme lengths, however, we can see in the case of Panahi how Hegel's state policing can be manipulated to deny even the most basic of freedoms. In response to this conservative potential in Hegel's thought, Marx and Engels produced what would become the most famous equation of individual and collective will. In *The Communist Manifesto* ([1848] 2004), their equation of 'the fall of the bourgeoisie' with 'the victory of the proletariat' (ibid.: 84) divided society into two classifications (or classes) and defined their will accordingly. The totalising function of proletarian will reaches an impasse during the era-defining social unrest of 1968. In the form of protest and social disorder, will alone was not enough to provoke a revolution in society – but what did it achieve? What were the results of this impasse in collective will? Kristin Ross turns to Rancière's writings to provide an answer. Ross argues that while society was not entirely overhauled, the naturalness of its policing function was, at least, deconstructed. The shared commitments of people from diverse backgrounds, discarding their ascribed roles and challenging the functioning of things, demonstrated the mutability of a seemingly immutable order (Ross 2002: 24–5). This remark recognises congruence between these divergent philosophies of political will. While strongly opposed on many issues, all these theorists acknowledge that change relies upon an antagonism with the foundations of a police order. What must be clarified, however, is the extent to which will alone can have a political effect. By disentangling political activity from what policing activity, some headway is made:

> Politics is a matter of subjects, or, rather, modes of subjectification. By subjectification I mean the production through a series of actions of a body and a capacity for enunciation not previously identifiable within a given field of experience, whose identification is thus a reconfiguration of that field of experience. Descartes' *ego sum, ego existo* is the prototype of such indissoluble subjects of a series of operations implying the production of a new field of experience. (Rancière 1999: 35)

Rancière's definition is abstract: it does not specify the way this series unfolds, nor does it methodically illustrate the order of these 'actions' and 'operations'. Instead, he takes recourse to specific examples to provide illustration. We should understand this not as a failure on his part to locate the shared empirical operations central to political subjectification, but rather an implicit recognition that each political process is unique and that no predetermined conceptual frame can be strictly mounted on to events as they occur. This is the major departure of Rancière from the Marxian thought of Althusser: the removal of a totalising logic. It is a 'new field of experience' that defines the appearance of politics, so we must preclude any predetermined formulation of its appearance. As such, I will not attempt to further calculate the empirical dimensions of subjectification. However, I do wish to probe the potential for simplification arising out of this passage. Cartesian self-consciousness is not enough to constitute the fulfilment of one's will. Panahi's disagreement is a process of meagre efforts: the development of political subjectivity from the morsels of productivity available. Furthermore, while intentions might be specifiable at the outset, the actual consequence of this wilful disagreement is itself entirely unforeseeable. Nevertheless, these mere efforts produce a kind of impact all the same: a policing structure has been tested and a sensible distribution has been altered, if only slightly. As such, *This is Not a Film*'s documenting of Panahi's disagreement allows us to articulate something key to the politics of art cinema. Granting spectators privileged access to this intimate space, Panahi provides a compelling version of the abstract definition of political subjectification presented by Rancière. Like other contemporary art films, it is difficult to determine a felt effect in the real world, but, by staging the experience of policing measures, the aesthetics of politics comes to the fore. As an attempt to articulate the acute physical and psychological effects of confinement, a politics of aesthetics is also perceivable. Panahi expresses an inability to act, verbally and physically, artistically and, sometimes, emotionally. His capacity for enunciation is, therefore, not identifiable within this field of experience. Through dialogues (to the camera, with Mirtahmasb, through monologue), through everyday chores, through pensive deliberation, watching and waiting, through an apparently mundane afternoon, Panahi treads the parameters of his incarceration and shows them to be as psychological as they are literal. Imaginatively, strategies can be coined to test and redistribute these parameters. His strategies depend entirely on the reconfiguration of an artistic medium – the making film of what is not film. These strategic efforts are exemplary illustrations of a series of operations implying the production of a new field of experience and, as such, should be understood as constitutive of a political subjectification.

In what follows, I shall discuss two such strategic efforts. The first regards his attempt to 'tell' the film he was prevented from making. While he derides the futility of this task, by making the effort, he somehow consequently reconfigures the space of his incarceration and engages discourses on the ontology of cinema in general. Sites not intended for cinema are recast, producing something unforeseen and unrecognised by Panahi. In this first point, I shall demonstrate the ways in which Panahi reconfigures the space of his apartment, redistributing the partitions of domesticity into the fictional spaces of his unmade film. The second effort concerns Mirtahmasb's demand to 'keep the camera on'. This results in the use of long take cinematography – not an uncommon device, but contextualised in this instance within the frame of a specific purpose. In this sense, I discuss the uses of long take and the banal content it comes to capture in *This is Not a Film*, arguing that this cinematic convention holds a latent political potential. Through several key aspects, I wish to claim that Panahi enlivens the formal features of these scenes with a political potential – not just to symbolise his situation but to enact and reconfigure its aesthetic parameters.

Panahi initially explains that, although he has been banned from working behind the camera, he is free to act and read screenplays. He explains how his protagonist is from a lower class than he and that his own apartment is, therefore, not a very suitable location. He cordons off the small space of the living room to suit his needs. Since Panahi has claimed that the borders of his protagonist's room need to be tighter than his own living area, Mirtahmasb takes the hint: he replicates this subtraction of space through cinematography. The camera stays put: rather than keeping Panahi in shot, he is allowed to exit frame, regularly contravening the field of vision. We see this as early as the opening sequence, when he wanders in and out of his bedroom as answering machine messages play. While a set of visual parameters are clearly installed, thereby determining what the spectator is able to perceive, one cannot help but relate this to Panahi's own situation – it is a figurative representation of the limitations on his own physical mobility under house arrest. The remainder of Panahi's explication of his unmade film is shown in this way: evoking – not telling – the experience of immobility. Limiting the camera draws focus and creates a distinction between Panahi's relative wealth (the bourgeois apartment) compared to his poor character (she is supposed to have no more than a bed in the private space of her small box room). However, the camera's stasis takes on new meanings when it reappears as a technique throughout the film. Stasis becomes a formal response to confinement – it does not directly show us what immobility looks like, but just subtly implies that our access is denied by drawing a line between where a camera can and cannot go. Disagreement hereby takes the form of an formal reconfiguration of house arrest. The camera's immobility is the start of this, but in the subsequent scene (when he begins to frame the space of his screenplay's locations) this disagreement becomes more explicit.

This next scene involves Panahi using masking tape to configure a fictional prison space. The effort invoked here foregrounds a distribution of the sensible, producing an inseparable conjunction between the formal arrangement of cinematic space and the political rearrangement of a social environment. Panahi begins to construct the fictional home of his entrapped character. He re-enters the living room with tape and proceeds to outline a rectangular space on the floor, standing for his character's bedroom. He uses a chair to represent her window and demarcates the area surrounding the rectangle as the downstairs living area. Recognising immediately the difficulty in proceeding in this way, he introduces some footage that has been shot on his camera from the original set. The chair/window is, therefore, momentarily granted a privileged, indexical perspective, introducing a sense of realism to his performance. Besides this momentary glimpse of the original location, the remainder of the scene involves Panahi acting out the script through movement, reading and explanation, outlining as a director rather than trying to act in a sincere way. This continues into a second and third scene, and so on until the concluding scene, when he loses interest and states, helplessly and exhaustedly, 'if we could tell a film then why make a film?' Through the playing out of these scenes to the camera, he comes to find this process tiresome and unsatisfying. Much like the meagre possible options available as efforts, this 'telling a film' ultimately proves an insufficient way of illustrating his feelings about alienation in Iranian society. Nevertheless, the process has yielded an unforeseen but major form of change: the transformation of his home into a theatre. Panahi has established that his home is a prison and that he is trapped inside its walls, prevented from making films. That he literally draws lines within the walls of his prison (to signify the fictional walls of his character) is a diegetic acknowledgment of the relationship between politics and aesthetics. It demonstrates that, with cinema, all that exists between freedom and prison is a line impeding one's perception. Furthermore, as well as demonstrating an appreciation for the aesthetics of politics, he has also literally re-drawn partitions within his own prison. Originally intended to delimit his space and time to the banality of domesticity, Panahi reconfigures the available space into a fiction. Once the spectator begins to accept this space as the site for the demonstration of an unmade film, its originality as a cinematic conceit stretches into other transformations.

The insertion of phone footage from an exterior location introduces another transformation. This moment provides an extension to his spatial freedom that can only be achieved through these handheld technologies. Another is his descriptive presence in place of the physical environments he describes. His presence is instructive, but his body language and descriptions seek to go beyond mere telling. He strives to provide some of the lyricism intended in his script. While he makes the effort to exert his subjectivity here then, the performance itself reconfigures a political aesthetics of visibility – both his lack of visibility in society as a prisoner and his invisibility as a director behind the camera. Once we acclimatise to this form of performance – once we forget that this is a man trapped in an apartment and begin instead to focus on a director telling a story – we can attest to the reconfiguration of cinematic convention. Along with the immobility of the camera, then, we can include the recasting of the private space of the home into a public space for cinema, as further evidence of his political aesthetics of effort. These acts – room partitioning, phone footage, script reading – demonstrate a disagreement: a clear contention over the meaning of imprisonment with subjectifying effects. While Panahi is supposed to be prevented from making films, he instead films the performance of prevention. This in turn leads to altering cinematic convention – indeed, altering what can be considered cinema. The significance of *This is Not a Film* really hinges on this idea of 'effort', then. An effort is, in this case, exhausting and unsatisfying; but it produces unforeseen successes in the uses of the medium itself. This is not a film, it is an effort at making a film, which, by attempting to overcome the prohibition of one's vocation, reconfigures cinema's spatial properties and its temporal possibilities.

The second aesthetic of effort regards the film's most explicit call to arms: a moment of incitement to rival the most committed of all political cinema. It concerns a single piece of advice given from Mirtahmasb to Panahi: 'keep the camera on'. This phrase comes to contextualise the film's use of long take. The long take is a relatively conventional technique, common in both art cinema and observational documentary. It takes on a specific meaning in *This is Not a Film*, attaching cinematic form to social activism. As I will demonstrate with reference to a number of scenes, the long take is a result of the effort to 'keep the camera on'. Before discussing the first scene, it is important to first locate this sentiment in the wider political landscape in the Middle East at the time of *This is Not a Film*. As Asef Bayat (2010) has discussed, the widespread circulation of mobile technologies and social networking played a key role in the protest movements and revolutionary activity escalating throughout the Middle East in this period. Phone footage of events has worked to undermine oppressive regimes and incite collective organisation towards common goals. Such amateur footage filling social networking and video sharing sites (like YouTube and Twitter) provided the only source of evidence in the international media coverage of the events as they unfolded. The poignancy of Mirtahmasb's advice is telling in this regard. Late on in the film, when Mirtahmasb tells Panahi to always keep the camera on, the contemporary spectator of *This is Not a Film* cannot help but associate this remark with the concurrent activities happening elsewhere in the Middle East.

This scene unfolds with Panahi quite innocuously filming Mirtahmasb with his phone. He laughs at the idea of filming being filmed, but Mirtahmasb suggests he might be on to something: 'what might you have documented had you recorded the arrest?', he asks Panahi, before advising him to record everything from here on out. As he opens the door to leave, a stranger appears in the doorway. Immediately, having accidentally captured this tense moment, keeping the camera on has paid off. While this man claims to be collecting refuse from the apartments, Panahi probes him further whilst filming him. He follows him through the building and asks him questions about his life. This involves a claustrophobic period in a lift, where Panahi insistently films this man in close proximity (Figure 1.2). As they leave the building, Panahi is prevented from going any further. The escalating events outside are shown in the explosions and fires we see through the gates of the apartment. Since it is a

Figure 1.2 *This is Not a Film*: Panahi's phone camera records the elevator journey, altering the visual style and taking us out of the apartment for the first time.

national holiday (Fireworks Wednesday) this final image could be interpreted as violence or celebration. These suspenseful final scenes spring from the suggestion that keeping the camera on could capture something of importance, legitimating Mirtahmasb's conviction. The suspicious appearance of the stranger ('who does he really work for?', we wonder), and his movement thereafter, underlines the merits of this surveillant approach to filmmaking. More significantly, however, the resulting cinematographic style tells us a lot about the film – albeit in hindsight. The long takes arising out of Panahi's purposeful surveillance has been a constant throughout the film and it is only in light of this comment that a rationale appears. Mirtahmasb's advice provides an instructive pronouncement of how effort can be performed. His words are foreshadowed earlier in the film, without the help of a slogan to easily explain. Revisiting a use of long take from earlier in the film demonstrates how it functions as an aesthetic of effort and invokes some of the potential implications of this mode of filmmaking.

In attaching Panahi's long takes to a form of activism, I am aware that I may be echoing a well-known precedent from the history of film theory and criticism: the idea that long takes provide an inevitably progressive form. This idea originated around the era of Italian neorealism, most famously extolled in the writings of André Bazin, who tied neorealist long takes to a truer depiction of the world, more closely representative of the 'continuum of reality'

(Bazin 1967: 37) constitutive of the everyday lives of normal people. Without subscribing to what Daniel Morgan terms the 'standard reading' (Morgan 2006: 444), which tends to associate the medium of photography with a pure reconstruction of reality, Bazin's preferential location of reality in the long take over the cut is the most grand and famous of claims on the technique. While the substantial body of scholarship on the long take's relationship to reality continues to increase in volume, what interests me here is the technique's relationship to the cut as a form of censorship and selection, which is another form of partitioning what is and is not filmable. In *This is Not a Film*, the long take is the inevitable result of keeping the camera on – the inverse, of course, resulting in a cut: a further impeding of vision. The same goes for the content of Panahi's long takes, which shares a banal (but ultimately unproductive) association with many of Bazin's own references. As we see in the opening scenes, there is no reason to suppose any stylistic preoccupation being realised through these long takes; they merely present the inevitable outcome of the only available option: keeping the camera on.

The early scene of Panahi getting dressed for the day is one of the film's most peculiar scenes. In a film almost entirely formed of the direct address of Panahi to the camera, interaction in this scene is totally lacking. With the camera placed in a corner of the bedroom, we see Panahi getting washed and dressed for the day. Initially he is absent from view, and we see only an unmade bed. The phone rings without answer and Panahi's wife leaves a message about her day's activities. She is interrupted by their son who states that he has left the camera on in the corner of the bedroom. At this point, Panahi appears into view. After putting on his trousers, he picks up the camera and takes it from the room, jolting our viewing position from the stationary chair to his moving hand. We then cut to the kitchen. While these opening scenes are clearly expositional, locating us temporally (at the start of his day) and spatially (we are in his home), they are also strange when held up against the rest of the film. The lack of direct address and the current absence of knowable circumstances leaves the spectator clueless as to the meaning of these scenes. This continues in the kitchen as we watch the process of making tea and Igi's feed, up until he makes a phone call to his lawyer and the film's context becomes pronounced. In these opening scenes, only three cuts separate five minutes of footage. Each long take presents three banal moments without any obvious motivation, demanding that we focus our attention on something unclear. It is also very difficult to discern any implicit symbolism in these purposefully commonplace scenes: this is just a man getting up in the morning – nothing more. How then do we account for the film's opening sequence? I wish to claim that the absence of both action and meaning here foreshadows what Mirtahmasb will later propose. Panahi's boring morning routine is what happens when the camera is kept on. His son's note on the voicemail about leaving the camera on is strange at first (it is surely not common practice to film one's parents in the privacy of their bedroom), but it makes sense in light of what Mirtahmasb says later. However, keeping the camera on is shown to provide little significant content. What it demonstrates, however, is an effort to film all that he can and undermine the state-wide policing of vision and perception. The long take is, therefore, bound to the disagreement at the heart of Panahi's film: both filming when banned and not filming since 'this is not a film' – this is just a man sitting around at home.

The recording of everyday events through the long take continues Panahi's aesthetics of effort, signalling another thing that this non-film is besides film. However, as demonstrated throughout a history of films that are notable for their employment of the long take, filming of the banal alone does not constitute something beyond cinema – something that is 'not a film'. From Bazin favourites like *Umberto D* (Vittorio De Sica, 1952) through Chantal Akerman's *Jeanne Dielman* (1975) or Béla Tarr's *Sátántangó* (1994), some of the most innovative films – works frequently cited as examples of what cinema can aspire to be – make the long take a fundamental ingredient in their constitution. *This is Not a Film* can be read in this vein: an aesthetic innovation that reaches the status of ontological dispute; in this case, it does so directly. This direct dispute with its status as film reverberates throughout what we see.

The camera is being used to make something that we will view as film; that the Iranian state has certainly viewed as film; but that is nonetheless undermined by Panahi himself as something other than film. If we accept this proposition wholesale, *This is Not a Film* offers little to our understanding of the political potential of art cinema. However, if we note Panahi's contention over the meaning of a common object – a dispute over what film is – we find the essence of disagreement. *This is Not a Film* is 'less concerned with arguing than with what can be argued' (Rancière 1999: xi): less concerned with showing why Panahi's imprisonment is unjust than with showing the limits and possibilities of cinema through his imprisonment and, indeed, of imprisonment through cinema. The aesthetics of effort go beyond the readability of political messages. When Panahi attempts to 'tell a film', when he constructs a film set in his living room and when he leaves the camera on to film the day's mundane tasks, he is not only drawing attention to the social and historical determinants of the present situation. Rather, he is demonstrating the mutability of social environments in general. Each apparently futile effort to exert some sort of will upon this social distribution leads to an unforeseen aesthetic innovation: a reconfiguration of the distribution of a sensible arrangement in cinema, in his home and in the Iranian state.

What is *This is Not a Film*, then, if not film? Is Panahi simply referencing René Magritte merely to play semantic, deconstructive games with the government? Partly; but to adopt this perspective outright does scant justice to the fact that this is indeed not just any old film – a lot more is at stake here. The consequences of even attempting to make this non-film are, for all we know, life or death. Its success as a piece of political art should, I believe, be judged on this fact: its urgency coupled with its disregard for the legal case at hand. When Panahi disregards the limits imposed on him and focuses on how he can reconfigure the space he has at his disposal, things previously perceived non-filmic become filmic – the banal space of the home is reformulated into a space of subjectification. The apartment becomes more politically incisive than the most exhilarating of political thrillers or most provocative of propaganda. Yet, beyond the successful illustration of a complex theory of political aesthetics, Panahi's disagreement is demonstrative of a wider, continuing phenomenon, growing throughout Iran and elsewhere in the Middle East. *This is Not a Film* is part and parcel of a social movement that is changing the world as we know it. When cinema happens in spite of politics, politics occurs in spite of cinema. This is the paradoxical disagreement at the heart of the politics of art cinema and it frequently results in game-changing works that redefine what film is as much as what it is not.

CHAPTER 2

Larraín's Ambivalence

> [T]he lexical homonymy of the word resistance is . . . ambivalent on the practical level: to resist is to adopt the posture of someone who stands opposed to the order of things, but simultaneously avoids the risk involved with trying to overturn that order. And we know, in this day and age, that the heroic posture of staging 'resistance' against the torrent of advertising, communicational, and democratic rhetoric goes hand in hand with a willing deference to established forms of domination and exploitation.
>
> (Rancière 2010: 169)

As we have seen, for Rancière, 'political art would ensure, at one and the same time, the production of a double effect' (2004: 63). An ambivalence occurs, therefore, between the representation of political events and an aesthetic interruption that complicates the social message. Although Rancière never uses these exact terms, ambivalence is a kind of metaphysical necessity in his political theory. As such, it informs his difference from many other contemporary thinkers – from the universality of neo-Marxists to the anti-universality of the post-structuralists. Resistance, as he states in the above passage, is itself an ambivalent notion: our resistant actions are usually performed through channels informed by that which we resist. To avoid the trap of inertia, then, the question for a political art is: *how can we shake this undecidable position while retaining the ambivalence of the 'double effect'?*

Theories of politics in cinema have tended towards an outright opposition to the techniques of the mainstream. The possibility of political action evolving out from within a film has tended to demand didactic explanations, which would account for cinema's essentially ideological nature. Jean-Luc Comolli and Paul Narboni (in 'Cinema/ideology/criticism', 1971) coined a way of mapping ideological categories for every film. They claim that, to engage critically with its ideological situation, a political film must produce a disruption on both a narrative and formal level. For example, films might have 'an explicitly political content . . . but . . . not effectively criticize the ideological system in which they are embedded because they unquestioningly adopt its language and its imagery' (1971: 6). They are, effectively, referring to the well-worn art cinema mode of leftism in classical narrative fiction.[1] Comolli and Narboni's argument would come to pre-empt the films and theories of political modernists. Yet, as history has shown, the access to, and success of, such films in their grand, diverse aims was limited. The intellectual rigour of experimental, political cinema, advocated by such arguments, had the effect of alienating larger audiences – and, perhaps more importantly, exhibitors. These films were little viewed let alone understood. Rancière's preference for the ambivalent would seem to contradict such attempts at total severance from cinema's ideological entrenchment. By inhabiting the ambivalent location within the binary (the *neither-nor*), we can locate the novelty Rancière ascribes to politics: a rupture in the distribution of allotted roles, which thereby reframes the spectator's view of things. The attachment of ambivalence to political art informs my definition of political art cinema: these are not films that altogether refuse the mainstream. As I stated in my introduction, political art cinema distinguishes itself from the reactionary art cinema described by Comolli and Narboni when it addresses an expansive notion of community – of an *us*. Stylistically, then, these films are ambivalently, resistantly defined; they challenge *whilst* employing the language and imagery of the ideological system of production.

Rancière's clearest writing on the political aesthetics of ambivalence appears in *The Names of History* (1994), where he celebrates the homonymy of the word *histoire*: the fictional (*histoire* for story) possibilities of the archive (*histoire* for historiography). I am introducing this strand of Rancière's thought to produce a more fully developed engagement with his philosophy, supplementing his arguments on politics and aesthetics with those on historical representation. In response to the increasingly empirical shape of historiography in the twentieth and twenty-first centuries, Rancière claims a 'political contract' (ibid.: 7) ties its contradictory essence to the ambivalence of resistance. Negotiating the ambivalence of political aesthetics discussed thus far, this chapter explores how cinematic fictions of political history can capitalise on the lexical homonymy of resistance.

THE POLITICS AND ETHICS OF HISTORICAL REPRESENTATION

Published in 1994, *The Names of History* implicitly engages with the contemporaneous debates on historiography that were being raised by the 'New

Historicists'.[2] Perhaps the starkest instance of connection between the New Historicists and Rancière regards his 'poetics of knowledge': a way of approaching attempts by literature to 'give itself the status of science' and 'define a mode of truth' (Rancière 1994: 8). Challenging the influential critical theory of the time, Stephen Greenblatt regarded New Historicism as challenging the Marxian universalism of Fredric Jameson's writing of the time. However, rather than siding wholly with the postmodern inclination towards particularity and difference, Greenblatt was also critical of the absence of a universal frame in postmodern theories, such as the work of Jean-François Lyotard. Greenblatt's work was pivotal to the New Historicist dedication to analysing the 'oscillation between totalisation and difference, uniformity and the diversity of names, unitary truth and a proliferation of distinct entities . . . built into the poetics of everyday behaviour' (Greenblatt 1987: 10). Neither turning back to Marx's historical materialism nor away from history with a capital H, the New Historicists' vision demanded ambivalence. Yet, like Foucault before them, the New Historicists' distance from totalising frameworks tended to mean shirking the kinds of philosophical questions on politics that I view as central for understanding political art. Rancière's attention to both the ontological and epistemological relationship between politics and history acts as a corrective to this. With these theories in mind, I turn now to consider what we might call *a politics of ambivalence* in Pablo Larraín's *No* (2012) – a docu-drama on the Chilean plebiscite on Augusto Pinochet's dictatorship in 1988.

As David Harvey (2005) has argued, the Pinochet regime was a neoliberal experiment, led by those in power in the West with nil regard for the suffering of the Chilean people.[3] To focus a film about the overthrowing of that regime on the story of an advertising director (a relatively minor figure in the scheme of things, whose job embodies everything Pinochet's government stands for) is a provocative approach. Itself the subject of heated debate in Chile (due to its lack of depiction of the suffering and its supposedly unclear ideological stripes), the apparent ambivalence of *No* has been viewed sceptically by commentators on the left.[4] In contrast, I shall interrogate the uses of ambivalence in the film to argue instead that *No* intervenes in the known or knowable, thwarting the straightforwardness of historical narratives. Neither a picture of brutality nor an apologia for the regime, *No* interrogates the very ambivalence discussed by Rancière in the earlier quotation, offering resistance to the torrent of advertising with a willing deference to established forms of exploitation. Unlike political histories which exude 'political correctness' through 'historical accuracy', *No* thwarts the seamlessness of mimetic representation. In so doing, the film also invites further debates on the ethics of historical representation.

According to Phillip Rosen, there has been 'an intermittent but continuous production of significant scholarly studies of historical representation in film' (Rosen 2001: xxii). We might approach Marcia Landy's far-reaching introduction to her *Cinematic Uses of the Past* (1996) for guidance here. Landy stresses the importance of constructing historical narratives that make clear the discursive processes of representation, which, in so doing, must acknowledge that history is not just as it is written; rather, through its *writing*, certain social dimensions (such as the capitalist socio-economic system) are falsely made to appear natural. To combat this, studies of historical representation need, she claims, to 'offer strategies for understanding the forms this naturalization assumes' (Landy 1996: 14). Landy makes a crucial point: representation always, albeit to varying extents, fails to account for the historicity of every element of its fiction. When revisiting past events in film – events that are often emblematic of a trauma still held by many – there must be, I think, some recognition that historical narratives are discursively, poetically built. Historical art films usually demonstrate a willingness to foreground the process of selection involved that occurs in representations of the past. Going beyond Landy's New Historicist re-evaluation of the poetics of historiography, I am making the case that *No* allows us to consider the political implications that arise out of this ethical historicity. Using aesthetic strategies to delineate the distribution of the sensible employed in the dominant mode of representing the past, *No* is an example of a film that does interrogate the naturalising processes often at work in historical narratives. Such a delineation simultaneously includes those usually excluded from the frame. In *No*'s rendering of popular resistance in 1980s Chile, the discursive principle Landy associates with historiography comes to the foreground. A knot is produced between politics, ethics, aesthetics and history, providing complex lines of inquiry regarding whose story is being told and what is excluded from these stories.

Ethical objections to historical fictions are usually raised when a text does not acknowledge the discursive construction. Theodor Adorno's statement on the impossibility of poetry after Auschwitz (1983: 34) is exemplary in this regard. Adorno's remark refers both to the uncontainable scale (in both experiential and empirical terms) of such an artwork and the sense of inexpressibility in a visual or linguistic sense. The logical conclusion to be taken from such an argument is that it is essentially immoral to attempt to *show the unshowable*. However, when read alongside Rancière (particularly in regard to his writing on historical representation),[5] Adorno's ethical polemic contains the seed of a political aesthetic strategy. Gene Ray elaborates on the contemporary relevance of Adorno's statement, stating that 'to continue to produce art and philosophy in the old forms and according to the old conventions [after Auschwitz] is to be in denial of what happened and what goes on happening' (Ray 2004: 225). For Ray, Adorno's statement is more than a moral code; it is an urgent ethical imperative against conventionality in art. Indeed, the alternative that Adorno implies surely conjures the possibility of progressive art *in spite of* the hegemony of insipid representation. He is speaking specifically about the historical incapacity of art to have any preventative effect on the unfolding of atrocities: 'critical intelligence cannot be equal to this challenge as long as it confines itself to self-satisfied contemplation' (ibid.: 34). Through his 'as long as', an alternative is implied; art might somehow respond more productively to traumatic events. To oppose 'contemplation', an intervention would have to occur at the level of the work's form, agitating against the typically realist fictional mimesis whereby things unfold 'just as they occurred'.

Ethical critiques like Adorno's recognise that there remains an alternative mode of representing the unrepresentable in art through the realignment of mimetic partitions. This shift from mimesis to *aisthesis* – from the realistic depiction of a known event to 'the transformation of the sensible fabric of experience' (Rancière 2013: x) – has the potential to revitalise historical narratives, allowing unseen perspectives to be experienced. This shift from the mimetic reality of the noteworthy events to the aesthetic transformation of the sensible fabric occurs in *No*, first of all, at a narrative level. The film departs from the tragedy of the disappeared to Gael García Bernal's lone hero who is naïve to party politics – the ad-man, René Saavedra. While René goes to work for the 'No' campaign, he embodies Pinochet's regime and its violent neoliberal transformation of Chile. To understand the political aesthetics of *No*'s inventive response to representing the past, I shall begin by asking: why is *No* so concerned with advertising? Is this a film that seeks to silence what really happened, replacing it with more palatable, Eurocentric themes? For some, Larraín avoids the challenge of political art, opting instead for a classical, individualistic narrative:[6] 'self-satisfied contemplation' in a three-act structure. This popular sentiment from the Chilean left is summarised by Gennaro Arriagada (director of the real-life 'No' campaign), who described the film as 'a gross oversimplification that has nothing to do with reality':

> The idea that, after 15 years of dictatorship in a politically sophisticated country with strong union and student movements, solid political parties and an active human rights movement, all of a sudden this Mexican advertising guy arrives on his skateboard and says, 'Gentlemen, this is what you have to do,' that is a caricature. (Rohter 2013)

Arriagada's response is understandable considering this film seems, on the face of things, to be less concerned with the experience of suffering than it is with the boardroom. It could be applied to many laudable attempts at portraying historical movements. However, rather than relegate the film to simple ignorance, trading-in authenticity for linearity and narrative economy, we can locate an incisive social commentary that is far wider reaching than the plebiscite alone. What it shows us is never there for purely mimetic purposes; advertising provides a way of interrogating the strategies of the government *and* the opposition, invoking the ambivalence of history to demonstrate the ambivalence of resistance. This ambivalence affects the way events unfold, the way they are perceived and their tone. While this is often mistaken for neutrality or apathy and, therefore, declared conservative, *No*'s ambivalence instead offers a position of immanent critique, widening our perceptions on complicit actors in the mechanisms of history. Before analysing how this occurs in the film, I shall first expand upon the significance of the relationship between historical representation and ambivalence.

HISTORY'S AMBIVALENCE

As mentioned earlier, Rancière's *The Names of History* addresses the modern historiographical inclination towards increasing empiricism. The argument takes us on a journey, from the storytelling of Homer's fables to the statistical data of today's social scientists. This is based on the principle that, to account for the true reality of the past, greater empirical breadth is required. In turn, this demonstrates an increasing concern with democracy – an increasing concern with accounting for everyone and everything. However, contrary to popular belief, getting closer to something more quantitatively comprehensive is not the same as attaining something more democratic. Rancière argues that situating history in an either/or situation (either in a narratological or a distinctly empirical dimension) delimits history's political potential. 'History could conduct its own revolution, he claims, 'only by making use of the ambivalence of its name – challenging, in the practice of language, the opposition of science and literature' (Rancière 1994: 7). The ambivalence he speaks of is lost in its English translation. The French, *histoire* (both *history* and *story*) is a telling reminder of the narrative procedure involved in the reconstructing of an event, reiterating the benefits of story-based histories; but in so doing, avoiding the postmodern tendency to dismiss empiricism altogether. He refers to the need to arrange a space for the interplay of literature's subjective effects and science's objectivity. This space signifies a distribution of the sensible – a would-be politically charged site of aesthetic engagement, outside of the realm usually described as 'political', foreshadowing terms he comes to elaborate later in *The Politics of Aesthetics*. This, in turn, highlights the political potential of historical narratives. The historical text, by simply being 'historical' – by 'preserving the specificity of a *historical* science in general' – sets-up this possibility. For art cinema to broach history in a political way, then, it must construct what Rancière calls 'a space for the conjunction of contradictions', resulting in a collision between objective and subjective perspectives, as well as past and present conflicts. In *No*, Larraín revitalises the questions surrounding a supposedly closed chapter, implicating those living in the present in questions of the past and reconfiguring the voices of historical narratives. In *The Names of History*, the most useful passages on the textual construction of this space come through reference to the French Revolutionary historian Jules Michelet:

> First, [Michelet] makes us see them; that is, he makes himself seen to us as the one who holds them or has held them in his hand . . . thereby affirming himself to be inferior to the meaning that traverses him. Second, he tells us what they say: not their content, but the power that causes them to be written, that is expressed in them . . . The historian will show us this power, which is their true content but which they are powerless to show us, by staging it in a narrative . . . He invents the art of making the poor speak by keeping them silent, of making them speak as silent people. (Rancière 1994: 45)

Michelet's opposition to empirical models of history is a self-conscious attempt to drag history back from its proximity to political science, with recourse to literary narration. In Rancière's reading, we find a more inclusive approach to retelling history – one that avoids fantasising the realities of the poor. Poverty and suffering are as pronounced in Michelet as a stone cathedral is pronounced on its own terms in Victor Hugo's novel *Notre-Dame de Paris* ([1831] 1978).[7] To make the poor speak as silent is to realise an impossible feat; but he manages it through his singular form of self-reflexivity, exemplified in the figure of a popular shopkeeper:

> If there is no place to make Chalier speak it is because no one speaks through his mouth: 'He is the voice of the deep, dark mud of the streets, silent since the beginning of time. Through him, the ancient, dismal darkness, the damp and dismal houses begin to speak; and hunger and fasts; and abandoned children and the women dishonoured; and all those heaped-up sacrificed generations. Now all these awake, now they arise, now they sing from their sepulchres; and their story is of menace and death . . . Their voices, their song, their menace, all is Chalier'. (Ranciere 1994: 47)

Through his subversive use of tense and person, switching back and forth (first and third, past and present), Michelet's narration creates a second person: he stands askance, acknowledging his existence (like an ethnographer), but also implicating himself amongst the events (in the omniscient style of a chronicler). Michelet's apparent success in realising history's ambivalence has a great deal in common with 'the seer': the champion of Deleuze's 'time image' (1985). The seer (first seen in the first works of Italian neorealism) refers to characters who, overcome by the experience of war, 'see' rather than 'act'. We might broach Deleuze's seer as a mode of vision that follows the historical narratives of Michelet: a mode of representing silent bodies that is, at the same time, able to acknowledge their unrepresented silence. We can, therefore, adapt Deleuze's concept, articulating its function through Rancière towards a newly politicised effect: silence becomes a mode of speech. This departure from mimesis to aisthesis rehearses what Deleuze calls 'pure optical situations' (Deleuze 1985: 2). For Rancière (as he develops most explicitly in *The Emancipated Spectator*, on which I shall elaborate in Chapter 4), the viewing position is an empowering one. Departing from Deleuze's dichotomising of *voyant* and *actant*, seeing can become an act in itself – demonstrative of the ambivalence of resistance discussed at the outset of this chapter.[8] We might begin by understanding René in this sense: an apolitical spectator at a time of tumultuous change – a time when people need to act. The debates on the meaning of *No* hinge upon the way we choose to perceive his ambivalent, 'seeing' figure.

BERNAL'S RENÉ

René is a small cog in a large team. Yet, Larraín insists upon hinging the entire narrative on him. By focusing on a character situated between Pinochetist neoliberalism and anti-dictatorial resistance, René thwarts the absolutism of the divide. Attention is drawn to the complicity of 'the good' with 'the bad' through Socratic challenges to the 'No' campaign's methods. *No*'s refusal to reiterate what the still-suffering masses already knew, and wanted repeated, is reminiscent of the controversies surrounding Hannah Arendt's attack on the Israeli state in *Eichmann in Jerusalem* (1963). Whereas Arendt's readership was an international alliance of anti-fascists, Larraín's Chile is still embroiled in the remnants of fascism. The majority of Chilean people are similarly anxious to promote clear and direct messages of outright condemnation. Since Larraín focuses on an individual who does not clearly fit into the opposition, whose presence even mocks the strategies of the opposition, his method is fairly provocative, but it should not be viewed as an avoidance of the realities. *No* is concerned with those silenced during dictatorship, albeit in a less manifest way. To clarify, we need first to mark an important distinction between the ambivalence I see René as embodying and an *apathy* that might be read into the film. How does the unpartisan nature of ambivalence overcome charges of the apolitical?

From the moment René agrees to work with the 'No' campaign, the film is a lesson in how even those somewhat outside the fight are inextricably caught up in it: a demonstration of the impossibility of apathy in dictatorship. René is a returned exile; his family has been torn apart by dictatorship; his son is estranged from his activist mother; upon assumption of the campaign role, he is put under surveillance. Apathy is an existential impossibility: in dictatorship, *No* suggests, one cannot but act. Even those who elsewhere might have been apathetic or apolitical instead occupy a strange ambivalent place – within but somewhat outside of the existing categories. This point is exemplified in the scene of René's first meeting with party officials. The campaign manager has invited René to evaluate their work in progress, screening two minutes of military attacks on the public, edited for their allotted television coverage. At this moment, we cut to a wide shot of the room and find that twenty-odd people are gathered to hear René's expertise. These would-be government officials are angered by René's desire for 'something lighter, nicer'. The response to René anticipates the backlash to *No*: 'Do you think that what's going on in Chile is nice?', to which René replies, 'This moves me like it moves all of you. But this does not sell.' Do we take René's response as representative of the film in general? Are popular marketing strategies a necessary response to contemporary propaganda? While René does not provide an answer, he does offer this vital question, which subsequently provides the motor for much of the narrative. In so doing, René embodies the thwarting function of ambivalence: situated between the neoliberal monster and the progressive politicos.

All the reasons for wanting to win are condensed in René's pure desire for victory – their diverse motivations are liquidised like a consommé, boiled down until some sort of clarity is achieved. The visual style of the work in progress scene reflects this. René is framed in a clearly visible, uncomplicated manner; in contrast, the others in the room are regularly blocked from view by visual obstacles. When his feedback is requested, René is framed like a talking head – the kind of privilege we expect to see afforded to the subject of a documentary. When the others voice their disapproval of his thoughts, the camera turns away from him. The turning of the camera from his well-lit, carefully-framed image, towards the interrupting campaigner, produces a rupture in the clarity of the image. A window at the back of the room pours light in, blinding the spectator as the camera moves over to the new speaker's face. When in frame, her face is not granted nearly the same amount of time or care as René's. The camera shakes, struggling to capture a stable image of her face between the glaring sunlight and the edge of the frame. To her question ('Do you think what's happening in Chile is nice?'), René's response is again presented carefully. Avoiding the intervening lighting effect produced by the camera's movement before, we cut to René – again, perfectly proportioned to fit within the frame. Another cut returns us to the speaker, still barely visible through the light. The camera then throws us across the room of bodies – quickly passing sixteen people – before it lands back on the face of René. In this brief scene, the mobility of the camera affects the quality of the image. The diverse figures from the various leftist groups appear blurry and undefined in contrast to the *clear-headed* René. This is the first thing to take from René's thwarting function: his portrayal – through his dispute with their ideas and through the cinematography's manipulation of image quality – is clearer; his motivations are more uncomplicated than the competing, conflicting voices in the 'No' camp. His ambivalence, which states frankly the terms of their mission, highlights the obfuscation of intention within their ranks.

René understands that to fight using advertising, utilisation of – that is, what Rancière calls, a 'willing deference' (2010: 176) to – the realm of its creation must be exhibited. These politicians and activists are strongly principled people who oppose René's apparent disregard for the morality of the situation. Having set in motion a new discussion – posing the question, 'why do you want to do the campaign?' – the second function of ambivalence regards something less explicit: a cloaked interrogation of agitprop. *No* aligns propaganda with commonplace advertising. The quintessential example offered by the film is the catchy chorus of the campaign song: 'Chile, la alegría ya viene!' (*Chile, happiness is coming!*). The origin tale of this song begins with his team's research into *what the public want*. The conclusion they reach is *democracy*: that is, the American, liberal democracy memorialised by Thomas Jefferson in the Declaration of Independence. The form democracy takes, they find, is (the pursuit of) *happiness*. René hereby excavates what turns out be a very fine line between the mechanisms of political discourse and the strategies of pop culture. While the campaign team – and, one would assume, the art film spectator – associates the latter with neoliberal capitalism (determining the very existence of Pinochet as leader), René's ambivalent approach to this fusion again brings to light the complicity of popular resistance. When he originally discusses the production of this song, he explicitly rules out anything with a history of activism: no pop, no rock, no folk – he demands a jingle. He is counting on the penetration of the public consciousness with the strategies of advertising.[9] Thus, in this union of the political and the popular, the scenes portraying the making of the 'No' anthem offer a scathing analysis of the marketing of progressive party politics in general. Its mechanisms are tainted with the forms of its opposition. This repetitive, catchy slogan is at once the height of propaganda and the product of the most basic marketing methods. It is the most repeated element of hope towards something better – its hopes are limited merely to something *better* than the mess they are currently in.[10]

When we watch the creation of the song, its appearance in archive form, its refrain throughout the crowds of newly hopeful Chileans at the end of the film, do we not ourselves share the feel-good sentiment? Even though we have seen the complicit spectacle of the facade, do we not still feel a twinge of emotion in the collective celebration of democracy? In this sense, the anthem offers a dual function: both an articulation of capitalism's penetration of the political sphere and an evocation of the *jouissance* involved in that encounter. In short, *No* is not a light-hearted investigation into the departure from dictatorship; rather, it is the creation of 'lightheartedness' that is itself put under the spotlight.[11] The second, less overt function of René's ambivalence demonstrates how the sober field of radical politics is compromised by its own reliance upon the methods it purports to oppose but itself employs.

Since René personifies and highlights the ambivalent quality of the 'No' campaign, he raises an extra-cinematic commentary on the role of the star himself – that figurehead of contemporary Latin American cinema, Gael García Bernal. His selection as protagonist for this film might be viewed in a cynical light, recalling some views of his earlier performance as Cuban revolutionary Che Guevara in *The Motorcycle Diaries* (Walter Salles, 2004). While presenting positively one of the left's biggest icons, the film was viewed by many as reductive and over-simplified, as summed up by Stuart Klawans:

> What socialist realism could not wipe out, liberal self-congratulation may yet turn to mush. You will know what I mean if you've seen Salles's *Central Station*, the film that made Cinema Novo into something Disney might have produced; and you will anticipate from *The Motorcycle Diaries* a similarly Mickey Mouse Che. He's played by Gael García Bernal, the slim and foxfaced young actor from *Amores Perros* and *Y Tu Mama También* – not an ideal match for the historic figure, but a canny substitute at the present moment, when Che has returned as a trendy T-shirt. (Klawans 2004: 32)

García Bernal is described in solely cosmetic terms. This cosmeticisation of the radical icon is but a reiteration of the already occurring commoditisation in T-shirts, posters and the like. For Klawans, *The Motorcycle Diaries* performed this in an entirely unironic manner, simply continuing the process of merchandising. Whereas *The Motorcycle Diaries* unapologetically detailed some youthful encounters that apparently had an impact on Guevara's philosophy, *No* cannot be described in such simplistic terms. In other words, while García Bernal's previous star presence lends weight to the superficiality of *The Motorcycle Diaries*, the ambivalence of *No* affords a far greater complexity. Larraín is unsurprisingly elusive when questioned about his use of a star ('I just want to work with the people that could be interesting for the movie' [Lyttelton 2013]), so understanding the significance of García Bernal's casting requires a bit of unpacking.

Broaching the star presence in *No* raises two possibilities. On one level, García Bernal as star falls into a set of classical Hollywood conventions (just like Larraín's streamlining of events into a linear narrative with a single protagonist). Consistent with this would be the idea that a major star can draw attention to a marginal history, explaining Klawans's claim of 'liberal self-congratulation' – we comfortable folk come to learn about the poor on our own terms. However, it seems striking that, where before his cast were famous only in Chile (for instance, stage performer Alfredo Castro's psychologically tormented protagonists in *Tony Manero* and *Post Mortem*), Larraín chooses to cast an international star for the first time. García Bernal's star presence is essential. Aligning 'the culture industry' of Hollywood with the hegemonic systems that would bring Pinochet to power, Larraín mobilises methods of the opposition. As such, the star becomes an extra-cinematic symbol of the compromised nature of oppositional politics and, therefore, provides a key element of ambivalence in the film.

Specific images in *No* support this idea. We are often confronted with moments of excess, picturing García Bernal with no clear narrative purpose. Two examples worth highlighting are his constructing of his son's train set and his skateboarding scenes. In these scenes, his face is either framed in the refined form of the campaign disputes I discussed earlier, or it is bathed in glorious sunlight. Aside from the allusion to stardom, both scenes are superfluous to the narrative, save their minor development of the childish side of his personality. We might view this childishness as evocative of his idealistic outlook on the world, were it not for the jaded pragmaticism of his actual worldview (a concern only for what sells). Instead, I think we should view these scenes as intentionally superfluous: they stage the cosmeticism of the international star. In so doing, Larraín self-reflexively acknowledges the paradoxes of star presence. Returning to the initial question regarding René's character and its implications for the politicisation of historical narratives, the casting of García Bernal works to raise again this question: is *No* democratically providing a voice for the silent or is it simply profiting from an emotional narrative? René personifies a challenge to popular representations of social struggles through (1) the character's thwarting of the ethics of propaganda and (2) the star's stretching of this polemic beyond the confines of the film itself (drawing attention to the cosmeticisation of politics). The film is significant precisely for its departure from political history films that rely on bloody images of torture, instead opting for a self-conscious contemplation of historiography, its relationship to the present day and the political aesthetics of reconstruction.

HISTORICISING TECHNOLOGY

Beyond the thematic antagonism with oppositional politics, *No* frames its ambivalent approach aesthetically through a subtle exploration of cinema's own conflicted nature. However, beyond the surfaces of the image, this is endowed also with a second, material level. In this second point, I shall consider Larraín's use of obsolete technologies. Developing Rancière's discussion of Michelet's voicing of the poor, the era-specific, video aesthetic of *No* has a similar political effect. It is a way of speaking about the past on its own terms that potentialises the re-discovery of the silent bodies of history. Building on Rancière's observation that 'to thwart its servitude, cinema must first thwart its mastery' (2006a: 11), Larraín's use of technologies contemporaneous with the era of the film presents a political imperative to be contemplated by historical cinema in general. Larraín chooses to shoot on technologies contemporary with the story in the three films of his 'dictatorship trilogy'. In *Tony Manero*, every scene is shot as if shrouded in darkness; even the daytime exteriors appear as though unearthed from a hidden bunker. The effect is to reiterate, at once, the psychological deviancy of the protagonist and the doomed helplessness of Santiago during the peak of the regime. In *Post Mortem*, a similarly gloomy aesthetic accompanies the era of the coup. One significant difference between the gritty social realist lens of *Tony Manero* and the dull surfaces of *Post Mortem* is the haziness of the image in the latter. Lighting is often used to counter the indexical realism, producing a dreamlike image: testament to the surreality of the situation in which the protagonist finds himself. In *No* on the other hand, Santiago is no longer a place without colour. Immediately, then, if we trace the aesthetic development of the trilogy: Santiago appears, if not full of colour, at least suggestive of something brighter.

This development is indicative of the shift in the political climate of the era. As shown through the departure from darkness, *No* depicts an era of hope and possibility. This shift is produced through the change in technology, from film camera to video camera. While the mood connoted herein is only suggestive, there is no disputing the historical context of the video camera. In *No*, it comes to embody the infiltration of neoliberal commodity culture and its representation through the televisual image. To elaborate, I shall first return to Rancière's discussion of Michelet. While not grounded in any visual terms, I believe what Rancière highlights as revolutionary in Michelet's depiction of the poor has significant implications for the debates on the morality of historical reconstruction raised by *No*:

> [Michelet] tells us what [the silenced] say: not their content, but the power that causes them to be written, that is expressed in them . . . The historian will show us this power, which is their true content but which they are powerless to show us, by staging it in a narrative . . . He invents the art of making the poor speak by keeping them silent, of making them speak as silent people. (Rancière 1994: 45)

For Rancière, Michelet 'invents' a way of describing the futility of representing a traumatic event directly, instead demanding a method for mobilising the exploited subject's silence: not the reconstruction of immobility, but a poetic, metaphysical elaboration of that experience. Representing the visibility of the invisible is a major theme for many film theorists that have engaged with fictions that deal with contested histories. Hila Shachar has demonstrated the way feminine silence is attached to historiographical silencing in *The Edge of Love* (John Maybury, 2008). Broaching a controversial intercut between a woman in labour and a soldier having a leg amputated, Shachar claims that what has been perceived as 'inhuman' representation is in fact an acknowledgement of 'the unknown and forgotten individual's plight in the face of historical events and circumstances. [T]he audience is in fact alerted to Maybury's scathing criticism of the consequences of history and what is left out of official historical representation' (Shachar 2013: 212). While graphic bodily trauma is repulsive to one critic, Shachar finds in it a way of invoking absences in official histories. The tension evoked between the war and the relatively minor narrative of childbirth leads the spectator outwards, folding in a web of other untold histories. Along similar lines, Marcia Landy discusses subaltern silence in *Black Girl* (Ousmane Sembene, 1966). The protagonist's employment as a maid in 1960s France renders her 'silent'; but the film's portrayal of this silence allows the spectator to become 'attentive to the myriad ways in which this silencing functions as a medium' (Landy 2015: 164). In both Shachar and Landy's analyses, the image of the silenced remaining silent – suffering that silence – allows the spectator to see for herself a denial of subjective experience in official accounts.

While in both Shachar and Landy's examples historical testimony is contested through a counter-narrative, *No* does something quite different. The lack of a clearly oppositional counter-narrative is an attempt to represent the silenced through 'not their content, but the power that causes them to be written' (Rancière 1994: 45). Focusing on the texture of commodity and commercials through era-specific technologies, Larraín returns us to the era itself not by way of the 'proper' subjects, but in a phenomenological sense. As such, *No* mediates the events in the way they would have been mediated had access been granted in the past. This has a political significance and it brings cinematic urgency. On the one hand, with Michelet's metaphorical portrayal of the environments of the poor in mind, Larraín's use of obsolete technologies embodies subjects rendered obsolete in official histories. Also, through its implicit gesture to developments in film technologies,[12] the film expands its critique of cinema's own ideological procedures – refined surface gloss is shown to be complicit with the glossing-over of the past.

Larraín uses the same type of camera that was employed to film the archive images used throughout. At the film's start, when René tells the room of executives that what we see is 'in line with the current social context', the visual texture of the advert on the television matches the diegetic world of *No*. There is, in this sense, a clear intention to ground Larraín's formal approach in the technologies of the era – not the content, but the texture of that content.

This goes against what we might call conventional approaches to rendering the past on film, which, while commonplace, always view things anachronistically. Today's digital cinema looks back on the past through polished lenses, with high-resolution technologies unavailable at the time. Of course, black and white film stock was not literally a product of the grey world it depicted; yet, in a metaphorical sense, it was. Since our images of the past are mainly in black and white, the contemporary appearance of a black and white image transports the viewer to a past era. To this extent, we can understand the historical film's attempt to replicate the experience of an era as determined by the popular technologies that recorded that era. For Larraín, this idea is central to his revisiting of Pinochet's Chile. Following Rancière's Michelet, it is a way of imaging not the content of the silenced victims, but the power expressed in them. This 'power' (what Rancière calls 'the true content' that the suffering people are powerless to show [Rancière 1994: 45]) is mobilised through the U-matic video camera. The U-matic was the technology contemporary with those 'disappearances'. The technological realism of Larraín's era-specific approach is, therefore, anti-anachronistic: it attempts to understand the past on its own terms. The effect of doing so is to show that film technologies are as ideological as they are material – that they are products of the same system of oppression.

To demonstrate how *No* so subtly historicises the ideological complicity of film technologies, I shall discuss two techniques used to highlight purposeful visual flaws in the film's construction. Rather than disregarding these as merely symptomatic of the film's naturalism, I wish to claim that visual flaws are yet another element of the films ambivalence: achieving a sense of realism whilst also self-reflexively gesturing to Larraín's presence. One such moment occurs when René first shoots the 'No' campaign's 'No-ews' (the news report format that introduces each fifteen-minute TV segment). In this scene, the real-life presenter plays himself, lending the scene a kind of documentary realism. In the pan that moves us from the mid-shot containing the presenter to the image of the screen recording him, we notice how different the presenter looks, having now aged twenty-five years (Figure 2.1). Larraín's actor bears very little resemblance to the man he is supposed to be playing. This jolts us from the realistic effect of the era-specific portrayal of events in a subtle yet definitive manner. In this moment, the technologies of filmmaking stay the same, but the artifice of the story becomes apparent. This artifice is Larraín himself, exerting his authority on the construction of a historical moment: the moment (as the presenter tells us) that dissident television can begin again. This scene broaches two important elements central to Larraín's and Rancière's politics of history. Making use of history's ambivalence, the juncture between reconstruction and the actuality of the archive is made clear. The spectator is, therefore, ambivalently situated in the space between

Figure 2.1 *No*: using archival footage and technological difference to contradict the mimetic realism of the fictional restaging.

the art of cinema and the science of historiography; but this technique also recognises the place of the author in its construction. Like Michelet, the self-reflexive formalism of the scene foregrounds whose vision this is – that is, the distance between the filmmaker and his subject. We see it again elsewhere in the film in the form of a subtle visual blemish: the recurring appearance of lens flare.

Lens flare is the name for those blinding spots of light that appear when a camera encounters sunlight. Countering certain critics who have challenged *No*'s aesthetic flaws as solely a symptom of the film's technological realism, I wish to claim that lens flare is not merely an effect in *No* – it is a purposeful, political aesthetic technique. This is particularly notable when René is first approached by the campaign manager. The two of them are outdoors when the sunlight affects the image: a bright white light-spot emanates from what is often (in 'professional' photographic terms) conceived of as mismanagement of the camera. However, it is not merely the quantity of lens flare in the film that forces us to recognise its intentionality; it is the careful, measured way in which the camera seems to create these moments of lens flare. When the camera zooms in from a distance on the faces of René and his soon-to-be colleague, the scene has the appearance of a fly-on-the-wall exposé, signalling the rarity and privilege of our intimacy with the characters. Not

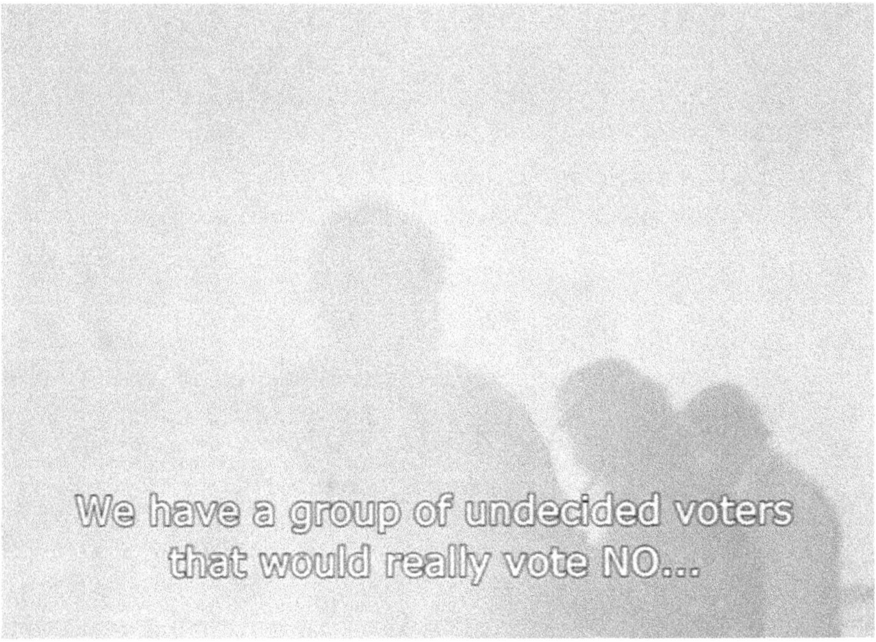

Figure 2.2 *No*: lens flare brings a sense of beauty to the image, but in an ironic way. The camera's shift into the light determinedly brings light into the image to acknowledge the artificiality of the film's construction.

settled with the two-shot produced, the camera shifts momentarily outwards, away from the faces, before panning back in to produce this bright light in the image. This occurs again in the scene where René's team brainstorm ideas on democracy. The lens flare here appears to echo their discussion on the promise of democratic happiness: a foreshadowing of the happy ending we know is (eventually) coming. It is in this scene that the 'miracle sized' proportions of their task are mentioned (Figure 2.2). This remark seems significant, in large part due to the use of lens flare. These self-reflexive flaws appear in the form of a God-like act, smothering the contents of the frame. Lens flare occurs throughout the film as an offshoot of the technology used. Rather than view this as an innocuous side-effect of the obsolete technology, we must instead recognise this as a reiteration of the ambivalence that fuels the film: artificially constructed through Sergio Armstrong's photography, symbolically foreshadowing the 'happiness' to come at the film's close. The topic of disappearance surrounds *No* like a topic made taboo twice over: in its literal covering by authorities and in its impossibility of direct representation. Larraín's political aesthetics offer a mode of showing silence, attempting to confront both taboos: disappeared people and historical silence. The disappeared return through the artistic use of obsolete technology and the limitations of the historiographer are recognised through the recurrent flaws asserted on the surfaces of the image.

'ÉL QUE NO SALTA ES PINOCHET!'

While there is an apparent aesthetic inventiveness that becomes central to what *No* achieves politically, ethically and historiographically, these techniques never depart altogether from the narrative tradition of art cinema. Each one gestures to the artificiality of the film's poetic, discursive construction without the iconoclastic denunciation of cinema that we discover in some of Adorno's followers.[13] Larraín's method of drawing light upon the disappeared does not deride convention altogether; it repurposes convention. It brings Rancière's remarks on aesthetic politics into debates on the ethics of historical reconstruction. If 'the dream of a suitable political work of art is in fact the dream of disrupting the relationship between the visible, the thinkable, and the sayable without having to use the terms of the message as a vehicle' (Rancière 2004: 63), *No* seems to fulfil this dream by recasting the distribution of sensible frameworks governing both mainstream and radical political histories. Larraín's ambivalence does not simply offer a haven away from the ugliness of traumatic history. This issue is confronted in the moment of the plebiscite victory. As the victors jump in celebration, René wanders home, shielding his child from the crowds, bypassing the campaign manager's speech for the television cameras. His ambivalence situates him outside both the politics of opposition and the success he played a part in achieving. Yet we know, despite his ignoring the chants of 'El que no salta es Pinochet' ('If you don't jump you're with Pinochet'), he wants democracy; he just does not identify with the party. This disidentification is synonymous with what Rancière defines as politics (Rancière 1999). As an approach to historiography, Larraín's ambivalence is a way of disidentifying with proper forms of doing history, developing instead a peculiar aesthetic approach to the disappeared. A challenge is posed to those who jump, questioning what it means to not jump.

NOTES

1. *Z* (Costa-Gavras, 1969) is mentioned, as is the less well-known, *Le Temps de Vivre* (Bernard Paul, 1969). These are by no means the best examples; rather, it would seem, these are two contemporaneous examples for Comolli and Narboni. Both films *tell a story* that criticises global capitalism, implicitly. The use of quite conservative aesthetic modes to tell a story might, in this sense, relate to even better known art films that employ a critical kind of moral worldview: for example, *La Grande Illusion* (Jean Renoir, 1937) or *Ikiru* (Akira Kurosawa, 1952).

2. It is significant that *The Names of History* is foreworded by Hayden White, whose theories of 'metahistory' (1973) play a major role in this theoretical field.
3. In his rich genealogical analysis, *A Brief History of Neoliberalism* (Harvey 2005).
4. Larry Rohter (2013) outlines the negative responses of those involved with the 'No' campaign in Chile.
5. 'Are some things unrepresentable?' (Rancière 2007) and *Figures of History* (Rancière 2014a) in particular focus on historical representation in the image. These essays return again and again, like Adorno, to the holocaust, as the exemplary case in point.
6. Encapsulated in the comments by Human Rights Watch director José Miguel Vivanco: '[Other important elements] were not part of the film at all. But I went to see a movie, not a PBS piece' (Rohter 2013).
7. The similarities between Rancière's reading of *Notre-Dame de Paris* in *Mute Speech* (2011b) and Michelet's method are significant. Both wrote in a similar era, on similar themes, with the shared motivation of developing a novel way for the representation of the demobilized and the immobile.
8. Furthermore, if we take the role of 'seer' as the lens for the entirety of Deleuze's argument in *The Time Image* in general, this complicates the way he distinguishes it from the *Movement Image*. The upturning of the sensory makes seeing an action, challenging the alignment of movement with agency. In other words, we might claim that the focus on 'a little time in itself' is just a different kind of action – stasis becomes an act. To see, to view, defines *a different kind* of subject to the one we find in the pre-war films he discusses in *The Movement Image*: one of static perception over physical movement.
9. The use of advertising as a sector that brings together both a site and response to postmodern consumer capitalism is an idea that is more comprehensively explored in the US series *Mad Men* (2007–15).
10. This shifting between *No*'s upbeat tenor and its fly-on-the-wall style (exposing the mechanisms of that tenor) are fuelled by what would become Chile's subsequent bureaucratic nightmare in trying to free itself of Pinochet's statutory mechanisms which prevented justice.
11. The continuing conversation with Adorno is again raised here. Questioned on the continuing relevance of his Auschwitz statement, he replies, 'it is certain that after Auschwitz, because it was possible and remains possible into the unforeseeable future [*ins Unabsehbare*], lighthearted art is no longer conceivable' (Adorno 1992: 252).
12. And, we might add, adding to the film's potency, this is a gesture to the relationship between historical representation and continuing developments in audiovisual media.
13. Godard's *Histoire(s) du Cinema* (1999) is an exemplary case in point.

PART II

A Politics of Cinema

CHAPTER 3

Kaufman's Dissensus

> The principal function of politics is the configuration of its proper space. It is to disclose the world of its subjects and its operations. The essence of politics is the manifestation of dissensus, as the presence of two worlds in one.
>
> (Rancière 2010: 37)

The above quotation (taken from number eight of 'Ten theses on politics') introduces the term 'dissensus'. A political subject 'stages scenes of dissensus' (2010: 69); these are not conflicts of interest, opinions or values, but rather, the event arises through 'a division inserted in the "common sense": a dispute about what is given and the frame in which we see something as given' (ibid.: 69). This means that politics has nothing to do with the work of existing power formations – it is about the ruptures produced within those formations and the communities thereby conceived from out within. 'Two worlds in one' refers to (1) the world in which we are interpellated as the subjected parties and (2) the dissensual – that is, *political* – world of subjects that will come to refigure that space. Since a Rancièrian politics need not, then, be abstracted from the more familiar realms of power, and because this relies only on the aesthetic manifestation of dissensus, we might begin to conceive not only of politics *in* art cinema but a politics *of* art cinema. To demonstrate what I mean, this chapter focuses on Charlie Kaufman's *Synecdoche, New York* (2008).

Synecdoche, New York produces two co-existing worlds: the real world inhabited by the film's characters and the fictional stage of the protagonist's (Caden Cotard's) new play. Employing surreal narrative events and manipulating the way we experience time throughout the film, Kaufman denies clarity and, in Richard Deming's terms, places the spectator in 'an entirely subjective realm' (2011: 195). The perceived reality of the protagonist exists alongside the relative normality experienced by all of the other characters. A number of shifts occur from the film's early, naturalistic scenes through to its intensified levels of strangeness, before soon reaching an entirely warped state, at which point the film comes to stage the existence of two worlds in one. Some critics (Hoby 2009; Deming 2011; Paul 2010) have been quick to bind the ideas raised in *Synecdoche* entirely to Baudrillard's writing on the simulacrum. It is hard to discuss *Synecdoche* without noting the significance of Caden's fictional New York. The similarities between Caden's story and Baudrillard's *Simulacra and Simulation* (1994) are significant. Consider, for instance:

> Whereas representation attempts to absorb simulation by interpreting it as a false representation, simulation envelops the whole edifice of representation itself as a simulacrum. Such would be the successive phases of the image:
> it is the reflection of a profound reality;
> it masks and denatures a profound reality;
> it masks the absence of a profound reality;
> it has no relation to any reality whatsoever;
> it is its own pure simulacrum.
> (Baudrillard 1994: 6)

Caden wants to reflect the profound reality of his existence, but he comes to mask that reality, mask its absence and forms eventually an entirely fantastical world that ultimately springs its own simulacra within. Like Baudrillard, *Synecdoche* is preoccupied with the falsity of what we perceive to be our freedoms. However, the implications of making this connection delimit the possibility of anything but pessimism arising from *Synecdoche*'s view of politics. Does Kaufman simply use Caden's unique perception of things as a cultural critique, reiterating the falsity of our lives today? Viewed through Baudrillard, the existing world order cannot offer what Caden is looking for and this sentiment is strongly apparent in the film. However, this cynical line of reasoning allows no room for considering the efforts Caden makes in the process. The question I wish to pose therefore is: does the film's use of dissensus allow for a meaningful praxis, threatening the existence of consensus as we know it? Or, is this just a 'puzzle film' (Buckland 2008), offering an illusion of spectator agency as a way of stifling other forms of more effective social engagement?

To consider the politics of an art film that does not broach directly the politics of the 'real world', one is forced to question the legitimacy of political antagonism arising out of conventional cinematic forms. We might in that sense turn again to Comolli and Narboni's argument and ask, do antagonistic narrative fictions simply 'express, reinforce, strengthen the very thing they set out to denounce' (1971: 7)? As we have seen with *No*, the ambivalence provided by being caught in the system can in fact provide an important catalyst for political critique, and perhaps change, thereafter. In *Synecdoche*, we find classical narrative conventions (such as linearity and psychological clarity). However, while narrative fiction constitutes the bulk of both Hollywood and art film production, there are defining differences between the two. A key contributor to scholarship in both fields, Kristin Thompson (1985) has shown how the classical style occurred as a rupture from the primitive style of early film, forming a character psychology through the illusion of continuity and the construction of a clearly discernible motivations for a protagonist. Thompson signals four key formal principles governing the classical Hollywood style: the designation of goals through 'visual representations of mental events' (ibid.: 179)'; 'character conflict' (ibid.: 181); 'temporal gaps to give the illusion of a causal chain of linearity' (ibid.); and 'overt narration to cover these temporal gaps' (ibid.: 184). For each of these four conventions to work, a spectator must be rooted at the heart of the action and relied upon to generate meaning (to understand those goals, discern the conflict, link the causal chain and relink the temporal gaps). Conversely, while the classical Hollywood system determines these formulaic principles, art films could be said to oppose them, governing themselves through an oppositional style. As David Bordwell has argued, 'whereas characters of the classical narrative have clear-cut traits and objectives, the characters of the art cinema lack defined goals and desires' (Bordwell 2002: 96). This mode of uncertainty contributes to some of the quintessential art filmmakers.[1] Yet other filmmakers no less attached to the category 'art cinema' have regularly deployed more conventional narrative principles of desire. Thus, to define too prescriptively categories in the art film would ignore the way art films are regularly in dialogue with classical conventions,[2] which might in turn neutralise its defining heterogeneity.

Taking up Galt and Schoonover's notion of impurity as a positive way of delineating its discursive space (2010: 6) and merging this with Rancière's aesthetic regime, art films traverse categories, staging then unsettling familiar techniques. *Synecdoche* takes up a similarly subversive approach, staging classical narrative and formal principles before tirelessly thwarting them throughout the film. This mode of staging and thwarting is not only central to Rancière's discussion of film history in *Film Fables*, it relates also to the 'double effect' of 'political art' (Rancière 2004: 63). As a scathing commentary on the perversity of North American culture, *Synecdoche* has apparent political 'signification'. The 'double effect' occurs through the thwarting of this signification – the complicating of what is signified through the formal suggestion of *something else* that eludes such clear explanation. To explain how this works, my analysis of the film focuses on two key features: the speed of the film's editing and the spatial qualities of the production design. By placing the manipulation of time and space at the foreground of this discussion, the frame of a filmic 'common sense' is delineated and the possibility of refiguring a world is presented to the spectator.

SPEED AND ACCUMULATION

As shown through the film's relentless drive towards an unhappy ending, *Synecdoche* is fuelled by a sense of hopelessness with the state of things and hopelessness in our attempts to change them. This futility is signalled by both the cultural preoccupations of the people in the film and the unforgiving, cruel nature of fate (dwelling as it does on the experience of mortality and the relative insignificance of our short time on earth). The film critically approaches the idea of self-absorption and the breakdown of meaningful connections to others, binding these themes to the impossibility of living in the present. This concern with living presently puts time at the heart of the film's themes. The first image we see is a radio alarm clock; a voice from the radio discusses the change of seasons. We learn quickly that the protagonist is suffering an acute form of paranoia, terrified he might die. From the relative realism of the opening, we descend into a spiral of diminishing temporal sense, until the apocalyptic climactic scenes. The intensification of narrative events through this chaotic temporal logic inserts a gap between the common sense and the sensible. That is, while the subjective reality of Caden determines the primary narrative, the temporal disruptions produced through montage complicates the grey tone and offers a parallel alternative. Speed, registered through the editing, becomes a reconfigurative aesthetic mode. From the breakneck exposition of the film to the narrative plotting and the dialogues between characters, everything happens absurdly quickly. Sometimes things have happened without the people involved even knowing. While only Caden perceives things as being too fast, he is distinguished from the uniformity of others. This is, of course, not to say that the white, male, artist has the solution to the malaise of consensus; Caden is a supremely flawed character, living with crippling paranoia, constantly defiled with embarrassing ailments and surpassed in achievement and confidence by his family and colleagues. Thus, Caden's perspective appears as critical as it is nonsensical: nothing guarantees the rationality of his perceptions.

The first scene shows us Caden waking: his alarm clock centred in the frame, he is blurred in the background of the image. A German scholar recites lines from Rainer Maria Rilke about the change of season and describes the poignancy of autumn: 'a melancholy month'; 'the beginning of the end'. The spectator is situated behind Caden as he listens, viewing his reaction in the bedroom mirror. This opening minute introduces the film's major themes: time, mortality, melancholia, self-consciousness. The pensiveness of this beginning contrasts with the sequence that follows it: a quiet awakening of the husband and father before he joins the noise of a family home. Adele, the mother, is busy attending to their daughter, Olive. She then takes a call from a friend. Caden complains about not feeling well then starts reading the newspaper headlines aloud. These opening scenes do much to outline the clash between Caden and his family: he is self-absorbed, unaware of the world around him, while his family are busy living their lives. This is confirmed as the film goes on. His self-absorption means he is unaware of the depth of his wife's relationship with her friend, Maria; he loses contact with his daughter; his commitment to theatrical projects separates him from meaningful relationships. Caden is presented as a depressed man, gripped by a fear of serious illness and, ultimately, death. He is a contemporary American updating of the narcissistic artist. His mind is shaped by the paranoid obsessions of contemporary American society (bound up in the ideology of fear and consumer desires). That we likely sympathise with Caden relates to his depression; he is not simply choosing to be ignorant of the world around him, rather he is clearly unstable. However, could we sympathise with this character based on his brooding alone? What possible political potential could the film contain if it was just another satirical commentary on the foolishness of the Western world? Surely enough of this exists already. Surely his self-loathing would be plainly pathetic were it not complemented by a formal self-consciousness. Without the introduction of high-speed (through aspects of performance and editing), the complexity of Caden's character is questionable. Increased speed of motion is used to go beyond straightforward social commentaries of discontent with the Western world.

When Caden arrives from bed to the kitchen for breakfast, several things are happening at once: Adele is listening to the radio whilst talking on the phone, Olive switches back and forth between the bathroom, breakfast and television, and Caden sits down to read the newspaper (Figure 3.1). The four audio-visual technologies – the radio, newspaper, telephone, and television – are involved in a supersonic interplay. The complexity of their appearance comes down to the composition of the editing, which in this case is sped up to exaggerate pace and duration. Conventional montage editing locates the spectator in an expository location, before traversing space and time to some great or small extent (across a room; across a century). The editing of sound and image in this opening sequence on the other hand is erratic. After the cut from Caden waking, the spectator is placed in the kitchen: Adele is coughing whilst making Olive breakfast and listening to a different radio station to Caden. When she then sees to Olive in the bathroom, the sound of their conversation, the radio and Maria's answering machine message collide. The radio, the phone conversation, Caden's reading aloud, Olive's cartoon: each one comes to overlap the last as their volumes are each adjusted in turn. The effect produced is to make apparent the abundance of information that is involved in what is really a quite

Figure 3.1 *Synecdoche, New York*: the hyperactivity of the family's breakfast routine is registered through an aesthetic clash of media technologies, symbolically gesturing to the high speed of everyday life and the subsequent accumulative effects of information. Even experiencing domesticity becomes an incomprehensible and strenuous task.

banal scene – a family at breakfast. While familiar to all of us that have lived in a family unit, rarely do we find cinema so concerned with the intensity of the aesthetic clashes when everything happens all at once.

What is striking is not the way Caden behaves, but the way this appears amongst all the other events. A similar approach appears in *Adaptation* (2002) when Nicolas Cage's 'Charlie Kaufman' appears on the fictionalised set for *Being John Malkovich* (1999). He is anxious and immobile amongst the fast-moving runners and production team. The scene provides an expository moment for his character, but it also demonstrates a visual and sonic style that will become far more pronounced in *Synecdoche*. Thus, while the subjects are quite unrelated, the speed of things becomes pronounced through visual and sonic partitions. These partitions become perceivable mainly in moments of clashing and disjointedness. This frenzied speed inevitably works to accumulate events. As we see in the opening sequence, so much occurs all at once that to perceive each action in isolation requires a technological intervention, like the manoeuvring of the sound edit through the distinct elements during the breakfast scene. Without this intervention, things escape our grasp, or simply do not appear important. For instance, the speed at which things happen at the outset affects our chances of noticing the man waiting outside the Cotards' home when Caden collects the mail. Even though we are placed over the shoulder of the stranger who watches Caden, we may miss him due to his apparent insignificance and our focus on Caden's own interests. As it turns out, this figure will play a major role. This is Sammy: we learn later that he has been stalking Caden and will later play him in the giant production of his life. We might also miss the addressee on the mail – Mrs Caden

Cotard – and its significance to Caden's later anxieties about morphing into a woman. The intensification of linear time persists and increases throughout the film, brewing into a predictably climactic event. Following breakfast, Caden is shaving in the bathroom. The tap explodes, shooting directly into his forehead and causing his head to spurt blood as vociferously as the water from the pipe. The blow Caden receives to his head is the catalyst for the hysteria that follows.

After this event, the pace increases, jeopardising any chance of the spectator comprehending entirely all that follows. The next twenty minutes contain an enormous amount of information: we see Caden being operated on, travelling home by car with his family, in rehearsal at the theatre, flirting with the box office assistant (Hazel), viewing his wife's work in progress, attending his opening night, attending the after-party, discussing the night with Adele and her friend (Maria), attending the second night with Adele and his parents, awaking next morning to be told that Adele intends to take her work and Olive on tour to Berlin without him. In effect, this is a summary of all the significant events in his life at one specific moment. Increased speed works to make events appear insignificant to everybody except Caden. Without departing from the realms of classical fictional conventions altogether, the intensity of *Synecdoche*'s speed presents a well-trodden cultural critique (if we live life at a breakneck speed, events inevitably escape us) from a peculiar perspective. Thus, Caden's perception of things becomes the 'division in the "common sense"'; but it does so with the primary aim of telling a story (from a highly subjective viewpoint). Unlike Panahi's life or death scenario, this is *just a film* – nothing appears to attach the formal complexities of the film's style to the potential for politics outside the cinema. Does it necessarily follow, therefore, that Caden's difference to what is an apparently uniform social order represents ways out of consensus?

Thomas Elsaesser (2009) has written persuasively on the use of characters like Caden in contemporary Hollywood, through the notion of 'productive pathology' (ibid.: 26). The term is one section of his thesis on 'the mind-game film': a contemporary tendency to reconfigure the spectator-film relation in response to a supposed stagnancy of more classical techniques (ibid.: 16). A popular archetype in the mind-game film, productive pathologies are representative of what Elsaesser suggests could embody a 'radical ambivalence' (ibid.: 24) – revealingly echoing the ambivalence I discussed in the previous chapter. The ambivalent figure escapes conformity, suspends common-sense binaries and urges consideration of the novel effects of social reconfiguration. Elsaesser defines these figures thus:

> Being able to discover new connections, where ordinary people operate only by analogy or antithesis; being able to rely on bodily 'intuition'

> as much as on ocular perception; or being able to think 'laterally' and respond hyper-sensitively to changes in the environment may turn out to be assets and not just an affliction. (Elsaesser 2009: 26)

It is this distinction from normality that invites comparison between what Elsaesser calls 'productivity' (both *for* and potentially *against* the consensus) and Rancière's 'politics': each one is dependent on the perception of a new way of being. Caden's unique experience of the temporal world he inhabits informs the way he interacts with those around him. He is pathologised, made strange and pushed to the margins. When coupled with the film's presentation of Caden's subjective reality, the mechanisms of marginalisation are made plain. This continues (as the title suggests) through the film's linguistic play with dialogue (which often mirrors the editing speed). Just as intense as the accumulation of time and events, dialogues between character are also fast, with new conversations often overlapping unfinished ones. Again, attention is focused on our perceiving quantity over quality, as the film dumps an enormous amount of information on the spectator with no apparent concern for her chances of comprehension. Elsaesser regards this confusing of the spectator as pivotal to contemporary Hollywood's 'crisis': disbelief ceases to be suspended (Elsaesser 2009: 16).

This is nowhere more apparent than in the film's representation of 'the talking cure', in the shape of Caden's therapist, Madeleine. Early on in the film, Adele and Caden visit Madeleine for marriage guidance. She hastens them through their responses, which suggests that she knows them in advance. That she is one of the film's main sources of humour says a lot about the representational capacities of the analyst figure for American culture. Again, this comedic theme (the neuroticism of the American bourgeoisie) is well-trodden territory. The surrealism of Madeleine's character (her name itself is an obvious allusion to the film's Proustian preoccupation with the temporal) goes beyond the Freudian themes of Woody Allen's films. Her first appointment with the newly single Caden demonstrates this. In response to his confiding about his loneliness and pain, she answers before he finishes his sentences. Such is the extent of her impatience, she sounds exasperated at his responses prior to him even completing his sentences. For example, when Caden tells Madeleine 'I think Adele's right when she says I'm not doing anything real', Madeleine interrupts with 'what would be real?', exasperated, with her hands out and eyes rolling. Her shunting of discussion towards her own predesigned destination seems to make her omniscient. When Caden reaches the point of deciding that he must do something 'real', Madeleine gives him a book she has written. We are suddenly shown random passages on pages in quick succession: the content heard on the soundtrack, the surreal humour of phrases like 'cats eat rats', 'vaginal juices', 'substantial crease'. In a second meeting, Madeleine again rushes through exchanges, pitching phrases about Caden's 'real self' in an excessive, pretentious way. She recommends a book (apparently written by an anti-Semitic four-year-old) about the snuff industry, with a protagonist named after several US presidents. The obviousness of the parody (disparagingly ridiculing callous forms of symbolic cultural criticism, aligning such modes with psychoanalytic models of interpretation) situates this scene in opposition to that clear-cut allegory: the film wants us to know how reductive allegorical interpretation can be. This is not to say that *Synecdoche* has no interest in dissecting the dark underbelly of US history and culture – these issues are at the film's heart. However, the excess involved in this self-conscious lampooning of allegorical poetics integrates the representational arts into its critical vision. All that is fast, all that occurs in the space of the therapy: this is highlighted as a constitutive part of liberal consensus. The events lived so fast in the family's breakfast, the attempts to seek help for one's psychological dysfunction, the representational fictions of America: as innocent and well-meaning as it all appears, the accumulative function of the film's speed designates it all as involved in the meltdown of the protagonist's subjective reality and as part of consensus. There is a recognition and severe critique of both the cultural rituals of Western consensus society and its representational modes.

Caden's final meeting with Madeleine occurs on a plane. He is reading her book and comes to a passage stating 'I am always with you. For example, look to your left'; she is then shown sitting next to him. When he tells her that the book is not helping, she claims that it is and that he is non-recognisable, as she leans over him and pulls up her dress to reveal her thigh. As implied in earlier scenes through the camera's panning up Madeleine's bare legs while they speak, sex is a powerful tool at Madeleine's disposal. An obvious distaste for psychoanalysis is apparent, therefore, both through the sardonicism in the representation of Madeleine's method and in this use of her body (her sexuality) to spur Caden on. Both function to manipulate Caden into accepting the vacuous nature of life. In this latter sense, the performance of therapy becomes iconic of the Freudian libido. The madness related to the American bourgeois reliance on therapy is laid bare: how absurd, the film suggests, that we should invest so much hope in the views of our therapists.

Madeleine's strange actions are accentuated through the speed of their presentation, denying time for anything slightly less bizarre to enter the scene. This sped-up presentation of their sessions makes Caden's appointments with Madeleine a surreal experience. Her significance comes to relate to the power she embodies as a prescriber of cures, embodying what Rancière calls the 'police'. Madeleine personifies 'the allocation of ways of doing, ways of being, and ways of saying, and sees that . . . bodies are assigned by name to a particular place and task' (Rancière 1999: 29). She functions to (in Elsaesser's terms) pathologise Caden. However, like the breakfast scene, the speed of the therapy sessions inserts a division in the 'common sense'. Roles are reversed: good sense comes to embody only nonsense. Madeleine's manipulative flaunting of her flesh in turn comes to reiterate the cosmetic character of her observations. That Caden turns away from these advances implies another way – a way out of the existing order of things. Each encounter between the pair thus stages a scene of dissensus whereby the patient overturns the law of the doctor.

Speed and accumulation offer a means of describing the relentlessness of change and the superficiality of our existence: we learn this from Baudrillard. The cultural criticism of the simulacra and postmodern alienation that defiles our subjectivity is evident in the film; but it need not be limited to those pre-designated terms. Kaufman's cinematic techniques enable us to fast-forward through events, explicitly showing us the absurdity of this existence. As people age and die, Caden is frequently lost for a way of accounting for these changes. His experience, like the spectator's, is asynchronous with everyone else's. It is in this sense that a political potential can be located in the film. By focusing on the mechanisms of marginalisation, *Synecdoche* addresses an expansive version of us-ness. However, simply addressing the margins is not the same as initiating a dialogue with spectators. In this sense, *Synecdoche* is certainly far removed from provoking political action. To go from the challengingly empathic mind games of Elsaesser, then, towards a 'political art', we might ask to what end the film addresses its spectator. The inevitable outcome of this high speed and accumulation of events is an exaggerated representation of the ephemeral nature of things. This exaggeration accounts for the film's comedy: we laugh in response to the absurd situation.[3] And here lies the point of tension – can laughter offer an effective mode of political engagement? To what extent does satire instigate a social disruption?

Satire is the most overt mode of comedic engagement with politics. As identified by Northrop Frye in his seminal *The Anatomy of Criticism,* satire is an especially time-sensitive sort of comedy: 'To attack anything, writer and audience must agree on its undesirability, which means that the content of a great deal of satire founded on national hatreds, snobbery, prejudice, and personal pique goes out of date very quickly' (Frye 1957: 224). Read in line with Kaufman's object of attack, the portrayal of undesirability in *Synecdoche* can only be conceived during times of consensus and might be seen, therefore, to inspire its spectators. To ascertain the extent to which the film inspires political action, then, we might ask: what is the force of that portrayal? What can be affected through the viewing of this attack?

In a broad historical reappraisal of the function of satire, Dustin Griffin addresses the conventionally bourgeois audience base (Griffin 2015: 139). Marketed primarily at an audience of art film cinephiles and produced in line (or at least closely aligned) with Hollywood systems of production, satirical observation becomes a vacuum for the free-world intelligentsia. Jeffrey Sconce has opposed such criticisms in his article 'Irony, nihilism and the new American "smart" film' (2002). Sconce refers to an array of films, which would surely have included *Synecdoche* were Sconce's article written after 2009. Sconce disputes claims that these films are apolitical and claims, instead, that their deployment of irony (both in comedic tone and spatial disorientation) fosters 'a sense of clinical observation' (Sconce 2002: 360), which he likens to Brechtian distanciation. However, to make these observations, Sconce groups together some wildly differing films. Indeed, starting out with the indie comedies of Todd Solondz and Neil LaBute, his claim arrives when he turns to Todd Haynes's *Safe* (1995), which, while ironic, is a defiantly non-comedic text. While the rigorous construction and political commitments of *Safe* are clear to see, it is difficult to locate in the 'smart' tradition anything beyond the nihilism he so disputes. His concluding claim states, '[w]hen such irony reaches the point of nihilism, we should remember that nihilism itself is not so much a belief in nothing as a refusal to believe in someone else's something' (Sconce 2002: 369). This is a powerful sentiment and one I would maintain, but the question remains: *where is politics in all this?* Where is the sense of interruption, of change, of us-ness? There is the danger that North American satire becomes a humorous but ultimately inert mode of observation.

If anything prohibits the satire from a greater dissensual project and prevents it from constructing a political community, it perhaps relates to the very determined socio-historical grounding to which Frye referred. So determined is the satirical text by its contemporaneity, its tendency towards what Griffin calls 'mindless cynicism' (Griffin 2015: 70) could be said to derive from its specificity and a refusal to imagine an alternative. In *Entertaining Politics: Satiric Television and Political Engagement* (2010), Jeffrey P. Jones approaches this topic in the opposite way. The critical nature of political representation in contemporary US television satire represents 'a desire to see more than one side represented', maintaining that satire offers an alternative to the news media's consensus response to the current affairs like the 'war on terror' and the economic crisis (2010: 239). Unlike Jones, I wish to question the effects of satire, not to discount its function as a medium of political dissent (even if it is to a relatively elite audience), but to recognise the inertia it consistently and inevitably invokes in spectators. A risqué yet safe space for critique is constituted, presenting the illusion of dissent with zero requirement of effort (in Panahi's terms). Since critique is contained in this manner, satire establishes one of the principle forms of what Steven Shaviro described as 'the feedback loops of normalising power' (Shaviro 1995: 45). In other words, convinced of one's direct access to political agency, the spectator is comfortably sheltered within the satirical text.

On the one hand, then, satire is a generic mode that recognises the hypocrisies of Western culture. Sometimes, implicit to this mode, a way out of the Baudrillardian deadlock is hinted at. Yet, in our laughter, are we not made complicit with the scene of consensus? Is dissensus itself woven into the consensual strategy of representational modes, diluting a potentially radical philosophy of social change into a mere vision and nothing more? This takes us to one of the key political impasses of art cinema in general: when formal innovation meets cultural critique, a redistribution of the sensible occurs and makes possible subsequent changes outside of the cinema. However, with nothing more at stake than the unfolding of a fiction and a hope for spectator response, the limits of cinema's political potential are reinscribed. I shall turn to the film's spatial arrangements to test further the political stakes of Kaufman's dissensus.

SPATIAL FIGURATIONS

Rancière reminds us that politics is aesthetic; it is determined by spatial configurations and exclusions: what is seen and not seen, who is heard and not heard, what is sensical and not sensical. While this perceptual law governs one's experience of a work of art, aesthetics in this sense refers broadly to the configuration of all that is perceivable – the arrangement and partitioning of elements into a social order of perception. We can locate this configurative ordering in the aforementioned therapy session. Caden occupies a familiar position: on the couch, adjacent to the master in her chair. Dissensus occurs by way of intervening into this logic (the reconfiguration of Caden's mental stability). The critical dissensus of the film's hyperactive speed disrupts the normality of this configuration and inserts a division in the common sense. As Madeleine ascends a staircase to retrieve a book for her patient, her higher position asserts a further, figurative value to the spatial distribution in the mise en scène. While the social is a collection of aesthetic configurations, works of art (a category distinct from the aesthetic) often entail the utilisation of figurative associations like these; but figuration is still determined by a spatial, aesthetic arrangement. A figurative image stands for something when it resigns its material function over to another (invisible, abstract) body. In this sense, Madeleine on the stairs stands for the power of the doctor. This a good starting point to discuss what I shall refer to as *spatial figuration*: the figurative capacity of the *mise en scène*. Throughout the film, images are formatted into a recognisable configuration to suit a particular, narrative purpose; but these images acquire a figurative dimension beyond that original configuration. Like the use of high-speed and accumulation, meaning is at once represented and thwarted, with the effect of evoking something else beyond the original representation.

As implied by the film's title, *Synecdoche* is concerned with the distinction between the figurative and the configurative. Crucially for this discussion, though, is the possibility that the film shows us the process of going from the figurative to the *reconfigurative*. Left alone with an urge to create a masterpiece, Caden constructs a gigantic stage that duplicates Manhattan. In turn, the stage directions he gives to his cast stem directly from his own recent experiences. He believes he is configuring a like-for-like copy of the world to better understand it through art. However – as he demonstrates through his compulsive, neurotic tendency of churning out potential titles for the play – he frequently voices a desire for this realistic imitation to stand for 'something else'. Consider, for instance, one of his suggestions for a play title: *Infectious Diseases in Cattle* (an allegory reminiscent of Orwell). The most extreme single instance of figuration must be Hazel's (the box office assistant's) burning house.[4] It signals the point at which nothing in the film can be taken at face value any longer. Asked about the meaning of Hazel's house (aflame throughout the film), Kaufman replies:

> I like for people to figure things out for themselves. It's not like I have the right answer, but if I have a visceral reaction to something, I'm sure that other people will, too. And there are a lot of different things you can react to. It's like a Rorschach kind of thing. I try when I'm writing to leave enough 'space' for people to have their own interpretation, and not to direct it toward one conclusion. (Kaufman interviewed in 2008; in Abeel 2011)

By singling out these moments as 'visceral', he sets these moments apart from the rest of the narrative. The 'space' he refers to subscribes to the same Romantic philosophy of aesthetics that influences Rancière's ideas. Both the 'free play of the imagination', which is so vital in Kant's aesthetics, and the 'aesthetic state' of Schiller's *Aesthetic Education,* indicate a form of training one's perception to experience the world for all its sensible peculiarity. The form of the artwork and the forming of one's political subjectivity thus appear synchronously. In one sense, by attempting to create a world devoted to the exhaustive detailing of a reality, Caden is in the process of carrying out this training of the senses. Like the cultured spectator of the satire, then, the art cinema spectator has an obligation to decode his metaphors. To remain here, however, prevents the location of any political potential in the film. The coding and decoding of visual metaphors establishes the film's 'mind game' with the effect of establishing a diegetic puzzle: the feedback loop of art cinema's normative aesthetic procedures. However, since Kaufman 'leaves enough space' for interpretation, the possibility remains for the spectator to interpret things differently, undetermined by the apparent code. While Hazel's burning house contains numerous possible analogies and potential avenues of thought, both for expanding upon and diverging from my argument, its insertion is a MacGuffin. It allows us to dissociate a relatively conservative mode that designates a space for 'free thinking' from a more radical, freer association with the image. The burning house acts as a way of switching on the spectator to figuration, exciting a less constrained mode of what he calls 'interpretation', thereafter. To argue that other less overt spaces for free thought exist in the film, therefore, is to suggest that the images provide opportunities not readily available through a satire-based reading.

To some extent, the sort of subjectivism this figuration invites discounts any single, preferred analysis. Yet, while we may use this as an interesting 'space' for discussion away from the terms set by the narrative, it is worthwhile to test Kaufman's 'visceral reaction' on a number of scenes that remain tied more obviously into the narrative. Since dissensus requires a dispute of not merely what is given, but also the frame *within which* something is given, we need to ask: *where in the film does the mise en scène imply something else beyond what is already being represented?* And, beyond this: *how do such moments contest the immediately apparent themes and offer alternative avenues of thought?* I shall revisit two scenes that appear to show Caden as a prisoner to his tortuous reality, but which, through their spatial figuration, imply the possibility of two worlds in one.

My first example regards a trope Kaufman repeats from the staging of his earlier films: the spatial figuration of the brain. One of a series of medical appointments Caden is told to attend, the neurologist appointment is staged using a meticulously weird and suggestive production design that directs the spectator in new interpretive directions, mapping Caden's bodily design onto the surface of the film's set. This technique has been used in earlier Kaufman films, too. In *Eternal Sunshine of the Spotless Mind* (Michel Gondry, 2004), a man rues his decision to have his memory systematically deleted and desperately tries to reclaim those memories. In one scene, the man wanders hallways, revisiting past moments. The hallways are structured like the neural pathways of his brain, presenting a spatial figuration between the built and the bodily. By holding up simultaneously the configurative (literally, one's brain) with the figurative (*like* one's brain), an interesting paradox occurs. The film's apparently banal spaces attain a significance beyond their face value, formulating incisive metaphors. Applying the schizoanalytic methods of Deleuze and Guattari, Patricia Pisters has broached similar techniques in recent films that focus on the 'delirious and intelligent, caught up in the vortex of . . . assemblages of power, capital, and transnational movements of peoples, goods and information' (Pisters 2012: 2). What Pisters terms the 'neuroimage' refers to the connection these films forge between the dysfunctional brain and the mechanisms of neoliberal capitalism. *Synecdoche* could itself be viewed as a neuroimage. Indeed, my take on Kaufman's spatial figurations employs a similar method, attaching mental *descent* away from reality to social *dissent* into that reality. In *Eternal Sunshine,* the protagonist's mobility within his brain counters the supposed immobility of his memory.

This spatial figuration also appears in the earlier *Being John Malkovich* (Spike Jonze, 1999). The entry point to the brain of the eponymous star is arrived at through pathways embodied by mundane corridors (like those in *Eternal Sunshine*), which take the form of the hallways found between offices in a workplace. While my approach to the spatial figuration of the brain mirrors Pisters' neuroimage, I would like to suggest that the meaning of these figurations can be more purposefully and strategically shaped than Deleuze's proclamation that cinema gives us 'a reason to believe in the world' (Pisters 2012: 5). Of what, for instance, does this belief consist? What comes of it? Are there greater stakes, perhaps relating to the conveying and realising of dissensus? To consider this question further, I turn to moments in *Synecdoche* when Caden's intellect becomes prohibited. The first involves the moments leading up to Caden's neurology results; the second refers to the initial rehearsals for his major production.

The scene of Caden's neurologist appointment follows several other appointments treating his general head area (an optometrist; a dentist). This has the effect of showing him in rapid physical decline. However, the realism of the earlier healthcare settings is displaced this time by a surreal, dreamlike portrayal: he is surrounded by bright yellow hall, with vast cinderblock walls, making this appear more like a factory than a hospital. The set-up is otherwise a bland doctor's waiting area: a life-support machine bleeps while he sits, reiterating the monotony but sobriety of the situation. The combination of un-real colouring and dull bleeping creates the possibility that what we are seeing is Caden's comatose state, the images and life-support machine sounds evoking Caden's dream state. While waiting, he reads a magazine that profiles his wife, Adele, and her new show in Berlin. As he reads, a nurse calls him in to his appointment, the camera cutting to show us a corridor leading away from the waiting area. This cut-away shows us a wide-shot of where Caden is seated, giving us a greater view of his surroundings (we see an arrow, labelled 'TO POWER CENTRAL'). These images present, at once, a figuration of Caden's psychical and physical brain activity.

Reading about Adele stimulates his brain activity and directs him away down the pathway to another zone. The nurse who has collected him is an electronic signal, redirecting him through the neural pathway. This is underlined by her unceasing movement when leading him beyond the doctor's office, before disappearing out of frame. Her soulless figure evokes the inhuman mood of the hospital, compounded further still by the doctor's assessment. Once inside the doctor's office – labelled from outside as the undeniably Kafkaesque 'Department of Evaluative Services' – the doctor speaks only in medical jargon, with no regard for the magnitude of his observations. He tells Caden that he will lose the ability to perform basic biological functions, like crying or salivating. Finally, he suggests they attempt a 'manual override' of

Caden's 'system'. The dire diagnosis, inhuman mood and Kafka references all imply an impending doom. Like Josef K. from *The Trial* (which Hazel had earlier been discussing with Caden) (Kafka 1925), he is aware of the spiralling accumulation of obstacles that prevent him from escaping. Nevertheless, as in *Eternal Sunshine,* the figuration of the brain places Caden in a paradoxically conflicted and emancipatory location. Caden occupies this neural landscape and follows the path dictated by doctors and nurses, but also functions as a figure of relative normality. Implicitly switching the terms of sanity, this sequence repeats the overturning of the patient/doctor configuration we saw earlier with Madeleine.

Once we recognise Caden's activity within these confines, we can also recognise further ways Caden begins to undermine the apparent limitations. These become clearer when he begins to develop his gigantic theatre. While Deming describes this simulacrum as 'too literal' (2011: 205), its configuration arises out of impossible circumstances. This defines the tension on which the narrative will eventually hinge: he is realising an unrealisable world. As much as the Baudrillardian simulacrum appears to be staged here, therefore, dissensus might be a stronger way of approaching this tension since it recognises the existence of two worlds (the homogeneous and the heterogeneous) in one. While the seemingly inexhaustible MacArthur grant allows him to realise the breadth of his imagination, the *mise en scène* offers a conflicting picture of things. To explore further the political aesthetic of spatial figuration in the film, I refer now to the first production meeting. This meeting takes place in a weird location: while unnamed, the framing walls suggest something like a locker room. Besides the obvious strangeness of the choice of location, it is also an extremely tight space, barely fit to house the fifty bodies trapped inside (Figure 3.2). Most are seated, cramped one behind another; some stand around the edge of those seated. Nobody appears fazed, however; all are hooked on Caden's every morbid word as he describes his bleak motivations. In the second meeting (the first rehearsal) the centre of the locker room opens out on to a space for rehearsal; the rest of the cast are seated around the edge. The single prop in the centre of the room completes the austerity of the setting: just a table for Claire's performance as the box office assistant. The result of this material clash – between access to endless resources and opting for hardly anything – mirrors the clash between the Baudrillardian analogies of the narrative and Caden's dissensual effort towards political subjectivity. It is here, in the film's staging of a scene of effort (in ways remarkably like Panahi's in *This is Not a Film*) that the film comes closest to making a case for the mutability of the seemingly immutable.

As the production goes on, the construction of his simulacrum begins, eventually descending into an uncontrollable city of its own. In the closing scenes, we hear doomsday alarms. This is never explained – these events

Figure 3.2 *Synecdoche, New York*: the rehearsal space for Caden's play exists in tight confines, emblematic of the film's concern with creatively antagonising with both material and immaterial restrictions.

remain in the background, never impinging on Caden's own journey. By the end of the film, Caden has confined himself to a single room in the imaginary reconstruction of Adele's apartment. The apocalyptic ending, where he is all that remains, implies that his production was a failure and that it houses no more than an onslaught of bizarre activities.[5] Caden is removed from all this: he has secluded himself to a small, unaffected portion, just like the locker-room of the earlier rehearsals. This continues right up until the concluding moments. His final walk through the simulacrum is guided by a map he comes across, labelled 'Warehouse 2', with deeper layers labelled '3' and '4'. His ultimate destination will be the centre of this construct, conjuring grand philosophical ideas about self-knowledge and self-consciousness. As he wanders through the devastated set, we might assume that his arrival at an absolute spatial centre might symbolise some heightened sense of self-awareness. Instead, he simply dies, seated beside a new, minor character. Yet, while creating another new narrative within the absolute centre of 'Warehouse 4', his ability to create persists. On one hand, Caden's hopeless search for truth has led him down a depressive path to nowhere; on the other, he has outlived many others and constructed countless spaces constitutive of what we might call 'new fields of experience' (Rancière 1999: 35).

Holding the tragedy of his story and depressive tone against the creative novelty of the spatial figurations, *Synecdoche* is always presenting its spectator with a difficult message: this is a sad, lonely life, but it is the life of resistance – of, therefore, dissensus. One's location inside and outside of the social order is what is required to realise the unrealisable. We have seen such paradoxes explored in the ambivalent territories of *No*. René unsettled the clarity of partisan divides between progressive and reactionary, good and bad.

His ambivalence demands acute attention to the neoliberal stranglehold on political rhetoric. In turn, *No* relays the past to caution about the future and it is from here that its political fertility derives. Can we say the same about *Synecdoche?* While *No* ignites a conversation on the ethics of propaganda through its critical ambivalence (being inside and outside consensus as a political and ethical demand), *Synecdoche* is more akin to lamentation (being inside and outside hegemony is a painful, thankless task).

CONTAINING POLITICS

In producing a film memorable mainly for its Borgesian conceit, Kaufman's narrative is bound to the trappings of Baudrillard's simulacrum. Yet, by placing characters who do not identify with these strange worlds, he winks at the spectator from within. This stages a familiar line of cultural criticism, which holds up the ignorance of our own imprisonment only to undermine the universality of this logic through the appearance of a marginal being: the dissensual division in the 'common sense'. Dissensus is not the result of Kaufman's critical view of America, nor is it to do with Caden's denial of one world and creation of another. On a symbolic level, we may argue that this is what the film implies; but in so doing, we would be relying upon conventional, narrative tools of representation. We would not be changing what Rancière refers to as 'the frame within which we see something as given' (Rancière 2010: 69). Kaufman's dissensus arises out of cinema's two fundamental components: the audio-visual image and its movement in time. When temporality is foregrounded and spatial constriction is tested, a space for politics is conceived. This is where the film is strongest and where its manipulation of classical Hollywood narrative principles is so majestically tested.

However, for a film so concerned with testing the limits of consensus, it is itself a little too neatly contained. Where the ambivalence of *No* leaves the spectator with something critical and open, *Synecdoche* provides an answer. In so doing, it contains politics, wholly, in Caden's impossible theatre: a house that cannot be inhabited successfully. While both *This is Not a Film* and *No* offer something up to the spectator (the demand to 'keep the camera on'; the tainting of the leftist chant, 'el que no salta es Pinochet'), *Synecdoche* is no more than a film. At best, it can be appropriated for 'political' ends – and even if this task is undertaken, what of it? What kind of strategies does the film invoke? I have contended that the film contains a positive potential through its imagining an alternative. I have also contended that this need not be viewed as an escapist alternative but, rather, that by altering the spaces and rhythms of everyday life, there is a commitment to affecting reality. Thus, if there is a shortfall in the political strategies of *Synecdoche*, it regards not its lack of commitment to reality; rather, it regards its tone – its use of humour to critique the diegetic realm. As I stated in the introduction, politically fertile art films distinguish themselves from the institutionalised art cinema when they address an *us*, a *we*, a *people*. Developing this definition further, we might locate an obstacle created by the satirical mode. The pleasure one derives from the attachment of humour to social absurdity is potentially alienating and elitist. Establishing a general sense of laughable contempt for the world of Caden's suffering, the film provides a cathartic haven for the art film spectator, captivated by the viewing experience, inside the dark auditorium, surrounded by likeminded intellectuals inside the art cinema. We have entered the absolute centre of 'Warehouse 4'. No further action is needed in this space. All are welcome, but there is a well-defined code of practice: just sit and await your final instruction.

NOTES

1. To name just a few significant art films in this regard, *L'Avventura* (Michelangelo Antonioni, 1960), *Memories of Underdevelopment* (Tomás Guttiérez Alea, 1968) and *Performance* (Nicolas Roeg, 1970) are all driven by the protagonist's lack of direction.
2. The French New Wave would regularly deploy self-consciously clear-cut character goals. Even the Italian neorealists (who for Deleuze, as mentioned earlier, realised a cinematic modernity that would come to define many key features of the art film) regularly hold clear goals (the resistance of *Rome, Open City* [Roberto Rossellini, 1945]; surviving in *Bicycle Thieves* [Vittorio De Sica, 1948])
3. When he learns that his daughter is tattooed, his new wife exclaims 'everyone is!' before pulling up her shirt and showing him a full-body tattoo of a devil.
4. After Caden arrives home from his premier of *Death of a Salesman,* there is a cut to Hazel arriving at a bright yellow house, situated within an idyllic slice of Americana. She is shown around by an estate agent as smoke fills the rooms. The fire is referred to only in passing. She lives and raises a family in this house, and Caden visits, but the strangeness of the fire is never mentioned until she dies – towards the end of the film – from smoke inhalation.
5. Including the strange, momentary scene of the military descending into town, inhabitants wandering the streets in gas masks and a naked, sadomasochistic old man being dog-walked by a young woman.

CHAPTER 4

Ceylan's Equality

> Political subjectivisation is the enactment of equality – or the handling of a wrong – by people who are together to the extent that they are between. It is a crossing of identities, relying on a crossing of names: names that link the name of a group or class to the name of no group or no class, a being to a nonbeing or a not-yet-being.
>
> (Rancière 1992: 61)

Contributing to a dossier on 'identity' in a 1992 edition of *October*, Rancière elaborates on the intellectual equality he describes in *The Ignorant Schoolmaster* (1991). In so doing, he foreshadows the theories of *Disagreement,* where he claims that equality is 'the principle of politics' – not its destination (1999: ix). Equality already exists in the world, it just happens to have been portioned out by and amongst the privileged few. It is, in other words, not an impossibility or even a wild hope; it exists omnipotently, albeit in a state of latency. Following the above quotation, this latency is interrupted when a visible body traverses both the site of visibility and invisibility, demonstrating the existence of equality and the 'wrong' of its denial. This chapter is concerned with identifying such a latent potential for traversing these sites in the viewing conditions of cinema and its hierarchies of spectatorship.

In *The Emancipated Spectator*, Rancière identifies two poles of political spectatorship: the techniques of immersion proposed and practised by Antonin Artaud and those of distancing by Bertolt Brecht. On one hand, the spectator's cognition is engaged through a spectacle of 'cruelty' – something that invokes an overwhelming emotional response. Conversely, the latter seeks to distance the spectator from the drama to such an extent that she becomes conscious of her alienation. Symptomatic of each mode's demanding critical approach is a stultifying view of the spectator: she is either too far removed from authentic lived experience or too much a part of the ideological reality. While theatrical in origin, both are commonplace artistic starting points for texts in the canon of art films. As such, art cinema itself has a history of treating its spectator in similarly patronising ways. From the immersive encounters of *The Passion of Joan of Arc* (Carl Theodor Dreyer, 1928) and *The Silence* (Ingmar Bergman, 1963) to the distancing effects of *Red Desert* (Michelangelo Antonioni, 1964) and *Funny Games* (Michael Haneke, 1997), the way the spectator is addressed can be questioned on these grounds. Nevertheless, each provides a point of discussion for the films of Nuri Bilge Ceylan: a contemporary art filmmaker who both continues and disrupts this tradition.

Ceylan is quick to write off suggestions that political symbolism exists in any of his films.[1] Nevertheless, when we depart from the socio-historical conception of politics (to which he refers) and broach politics as an aesthetic activity, an alternative thesis arises around social hierarchy that exists in film spectatorship. This is suggested through a general overview of the plot. Ceylan stars in the film, playing an academic who specialises in photography, going through a relationship crisis with a woman played by his wife (Ebru Ceylan). Since Ceylan is director, actor and almost certainly the subject upon whom the protagonist is based, it is impossible not to read into this traversal of roles something else beyond the narrowly existential themes in the foreground. Ceylan overtly draws attention to himself as the author – he demands we recognise his looming presence throughout. This self-conscious performance of the authorial role reconfigures notions of the auteur in theories of cinema and spectatorship.

In this chapter, I shall argue that Ceylan's traversal of roles in *Climates* instigates the dismantling of several aesthetic hierarchies and complicates dominant theories of spectatorship that involve what Rancière describes as an 'embodied allegory of inequality' (2009c: 12). Such allegories continue in postmodern theories of spectatorship. Barthes' argument on 'the death of the author' (1977) and Foucault's claim that 'the author function will disappear' (1986) influenced an era of philosophy geared towards the undermining of authorial value. In tandem with the strengthening of radical politics of the time, the outright abolition or 'disappearance' of the genial artist figure was deemed a necessary act. Across these examples, a commitment is always made to activating the spectator's thought. Whilst socially engaged and progressive, the role of the spectator is determined by, and thus deemed subordinate to, the intellectual.[2] The insufficiency of this account of spectatorship is noted by Judith Mayne when she describes the 'persistent duality of being inside ideology and complicit, versus being outside it and therefore resistant', which, she claims, simply reduces politics 'to a question of reading, and the complexities of spectatorship to facile and static opposition' (Mayne 1993: 138). We can, therefore, see how Rancière's assumption of equality offers something different, breaking with the dominant critical mode that presumes the spectator's essential passivity. What we lack currently is a method of understanding the way such an equality might be accounted for through a film. I would like to offer *Climates* as an exemplary text in this regard. Ceylan develops *The Emancipated Spectator*'s concern for dismantling the hierarchy of artist above spectator and searches for points of commonality where both can meet.

THE HIERARCHY OF SPECTATORSHIP

Hierarchy in cinema is perhaps most pronounced through the notion of intentionality, as expressed through the history and criticism of 'the auteur theory'. Proponents of this theory locate the artistic achievements of a film squarely in the personality of the director. Despite a persisting backlash against its proponents, auteurism's continuing popularity apparently negates a wholesale rejection of the discourse. This is a theoretical approach to cinema that entails the collating of canons and tastes, yet countless studies of film analysis identify a profoundly committed, social enterprise in many wholeheartedly auteurist oeuvres. We might in this case recognise a new lease of life in the study of auteurism – one that is not steeped in nostalgia for the ideas of André Bazin or Andrew Sarris. Moreover, working with the auteur as a concept – rather than dismissing it altogether as an elitist, conservative misstep – allows for further insight into Rancière's own focus on the canon. Since his own writing on film takes for granted an auteurist approach, little has been made of the explicit linkage between the auteur and the politics of spectatorship.

In Rancière's theory of spectatorship, emancipation is the 'third thing', which is 'owned by no one, whose meaning is owned by no one, but which subsists between them, excluding any uniform transmission, any identity of cause and effect' (Rancière 2009c: 15). There is no hierarchy of intention asserting the artist's primacy over the spectator's perception. Yet, because it is recognised that the spectator's perception is equal to – and not substitutive for – the artist's intent, the 'third thing' still carries the trace of the first 'thing' (the author). This is the tension that political filmmaking initiatives like Dziga Vertov Group and Black Audio Film Collective were antagonising with throughout their work, viewing instead filmmaking as a collective activity. Their concern for challenging social injustice began from the question of individual authorship, attaching ideas around intentionality to extra-cinematic social hierarchies. *Climates* raises such polemics in the conventional auteur mode of art cinema, which urges the question: can the spectator's equality be recovered *by* the auteur? Is the author able to incorporate the levelling of hierarchy into his own 'transmission'?

Tom Conley has used Rancière's theories to offer an answer to these questions. Building on Rancière's engagement with a film by Humphrey Jennings, Conley finds in *Listen to Britain* (1942) a space for politics deriving precisely from Jennings's emergence from 'a context in which artists and ethnographers organised a movement seeking to mix surreal and everyday registers of reality':

> [Jennings] sought to turn the observer or patent 'author' of a study of the contemporary world into his or her own subject, and, contrawise, to make the subjects of their studies authors of themselves and their milieus in their own right. Once the distinction between observer and observed was dissolved a rich field of contradiction and coincidence (of political virtue) became visible. (Conley 2009: 144)

Conley claims that Jennings's poetic non-fiction potentialises a new author – one that might inseminate from without the film itself. The reverse occurs in *Climates*, but it produces similar effects: Ceylan's biographical fiction instigates a potential new author by traversing spaces within, outside and adjacent to the diegesis. Like Conley's Jennings,[3] Ceylan realigns the partitions framing the profilmic space, the extra-cinematic space and the formative space of spectatorship. Several formal choices test cinematic boundaries, which, as I shall explain, work to acknowledge the existing equality between auteur and spectator. I have thus far made this claim based on the act of Ceylan's role traversal alone, but there is greater reason to pursue this argument within the space of the film itself in ways thus far unacknowledged. Existing analyses of *Climates* struggle to negotiate its distinct formal decisions with the narrative. Either plots are bound to sociological commentaries on the Turkish state at the expense of sufficient formal analysis, or the film's formal techniques are prioritised at the expense of the social relationships in the film.[4] Asuman Suner (2004) begins to develop an argument which binds certain formal techniques to social issues, but this relates purely to a nationalistic, Turkish people – not, as Ceylan has described his films, about 'humanity in general'. In this sense, none of the existing approaches pay serious attention to the political potential of the film's autobiographical, extra-cinematic dimension. Unlike the relevance of Iranian and Chilean social issues to the first two arguments, I am focusing here on how the politico-aesthetic (not the socio-historical) distributions of the film challenge aesthetic hierarchies. This chapter posits that *Climates* is worth critical examination due to the ramifications of Ceylan's traversal of various roles, including that of filmmaker, performer, and, ostensibly, the autobiographical subject of the film. By both installing and undermining this hierarchy of roles, Ceylan sets a precedent that would, in turn, appear to install and undermine the relation of power between auteur and spectator. To elaborate, I begin by turning to a scene Robin Wood described as a 'heroic' challenge to Ceylan's authorial privilege (Wood 2006: 286).

This scene follows an opening sequence that establishes the discord between Ceylan's protagonist (Isa) and his partner (Bahar). The two are having dinner with another couple; the camera places the spectator at table height, side-on to the four of them, never moving or cutting away. This locates Bahar in the foreground sitting opposite the other man, with Isa next to her opposite the other woman. The other man's wife leaves the table to make coffee. Bahar, however, has sat silently throughout the meal. The framing of this event foregrounds the disregard of Bahar (located on the right of the image) and her inactivity in contrast to the other man's (on the left) partaking in the conversation. However, when she interrupts the conversation, the scene takes on another significance. Isa's apparent embarrassment at her outburst provokes Bahar to say, 'don't worry, they enjoy seeing us miserable'. In the diegetic context, 'they' would seem to refer to the other couple. However, 'they' could also refer to those other bodies who are physically absent in the scene, but implicated nevertheless in the scenario. In this tableau image, the camera is seated at the head of the table, as though embodying the gaze of the spectator. We might, therefore, claim that Bahar (like Peter and Paul in *Funny Games*) gestures to the sadistic desire of spectators, wishing to view a relationship in crisis. The 'us' spectators 'enjoy seeing miserable' is the couple in the film (or couples in films). In its staging of interpersonal disconnect, a relationship crisis narrative presents a platform for the thinking through of film/spectator relations. Even without the inclusion of Ceylan in his own film, this poses complex challenges to the traditional author/spectator relationship. Beyond the self-reflexive provocations of *Funny Games,* however, Ceylan's inclusion incites acclamations of 'heroism': the author's own body enters the frame to make himself vulnerable and, in this scene, quite literally lays it on the table for discussion.

It is this submission of authority that prohibits Ceylan's authorial agency. This moment of weakness reinforces his traversing of the director and performer roles, thereby affecting the hierarchical relationship of cinematic role allocation. This staging and undermining of cinematic hierarchies occurs throughout the film. I shall discuss three such hierarchies that continue his initial role traversal. Firstly, I shall expand upon the aforementioned depiction of self-deprecation that weakens Ceylan's character and his facade of authority. Secondly, I broach the film's conceptual use of fragmentation, which becomes a way of recognising the equality of usually subordinated elements in the image. This is identifiable in the film's close-ups and the strange montages of images with no clear relevance to the event portrayed. Third, and finally, I consider moments in the film that confuse a distinction between fantasy and reality, challenging the authority of one kind of truth over another. As I will attempt to elucidate through each point, every one of these specific challenges is aimed at Ceylan's primary achievement: the enactment of equality.

SELF-DEPRECATION

This first point engages with Ceylan's self-deprecating character. The idea of undermining one's intellect in film for comic effect is not unique. In cinema, one can trace its lineage back to Charlie Chaplin and Buster Keaton – artistically masterminding the film as the author, but assuredly using the film as a space of self-ridicule. Rancière has claimed that these burlesque characters were 'constantly shuttling between total impotence and absolute power', thus illustrating that cinema is capable of 'thwarting the servitude that enslaves it to industry, if it first thwarts its mastery' (2006a: 12). The policing powers of industrial production, coupled with standardised modes of exhibition and reception, place a strain on the artistic integrity of the filmmaker; but, as Chaplin and Keaton demonstrated, this can be thwarted through methods that undermine the apparent seamlessness of the spectacle. The 'total impotence' of the burlesque body mocks the 'self' of the artist and, in turn, mocks the authority the artist embodies. As demonstrated in the dinner party scene in *Climates*, Ceylan's is a solemn reimagining of the burlesque body, achieved primarily through his unique usage of self-deprecation. However, whereas Chaplin and Keaton represent an underdog or everyman figure, Ceylan is an intellectual: his self-deprecating thwarting of mastery comes by dwelling upon his own pomposity. The most frequently cited example of this self-deprecation comes from his earlier film, *Distant* (2002).[5] Mahmut (standing in for Ceylan) has his cousin Yussuf staying with him, attempting to make a go of things in the big city. This produces a number of scenarios whereby Mahmut feels the need to exert his authority over his naive cousin, making clear his cultured superiority. The hypocrisy of Mahmut's own life is made clear in a scene involving the pair watching Andrei Tarkovsky's *Stalker* (1979). Tarkovsky – known for his intensely contemplative style – is mentioned elsewhere as a major influence on Mahmut's poetic approach to his photographic work. When Yussuf leaves the room, unprepared to tolerate any more of three men standing on a moving canoe, Mahmut switches to pornography. Soon after, Yussuf returns, prompting Mahmut to switch to more respectable programming: a kung fu film, which Yussuf likes the look of so much that he decides to stick around, which prompts Mahmut to go to bed. Geoff Dyer calls this moment 'the most deadpan I have ever seen in a film' (Dyer 2012), illustrating the difference between the kind of burlesque humour one finds in a Keaton film and the self-deprecating style of Ceylan. Nevertheless, both burlesque performances and Ceylan's self-deprecating deadpan have the shared motivation of using humour to mock a system within which they are deeply ingrained.

In *Distant,* Ceylan mocks Tarkovsky's durational excess; but Tarkovsky's visual, textural and tonal style is clearly employed through Ceylan's films. In moments like this one in *Distant,* threats to cinematic institutional hierarchy are brought about by undermining the cinematic canon (within which Tarkovsky occupies a sacred place). *Climates* contains several such moments, producing deadpan humour in Ceylan's moods, acts and gestures. He inexplicably rests his head in a drawer; he acts like an infant during a sexual liaison; he preciously agonises over his doctoral thesis despite being employed as a lecturer; he sulks throughout Bahar's phone conversations: these are instances of Ceylan creating pathetic images of Ceylan. Probably the most incisive moment of self-deprecation appears in a sequence that, like *Distant,* gestures towards the conceitedness of the artist. This sequence comes late on in the film, when Ceylan's character, Isa, is photographing some of the majestic landscape. In a taxi to the airport, he asks the driver to stop near a view of a castle. Having taken shots of only landscapes, Isa notices that his pictures are devoid of people and asks the driver to stand in the shot. The driver obliges awkwardly, unsure what pose is expected of him. 'Do nothing, be yourself', Isa says. Having taken the picture and returned to the car, the driver asks if he can have the picture, to which Isa replies, 'What would *you* want with it?' The sentiment is clear: 'what would you, a commoner, want with this beautiful work of art?' Isa can only be viewed as snobbish in this instance. Indeed, the preceding landscapes he has just photographed take on a new meaning in hindsight. Prior to this exchange, Isa's departure from the city for photographs of distant, unpopulated villages might have been considered a way of shedding light on disregarded spaces. Now, in light of the pompous remark, ambiguity is all but removed: these photographs offer 'proof' of his 'genius', beyond the understanding of the commoner. The lack of people in his photographs multiplies this – it is as though commoners must not soil his beautiful landscapes. The exchange with the taxi driver is the only scene in the film where we see Isa interacting with someone outside of his immediate family and peers. Even though it is a fleeting remark, it has great ramifications on the image Ceylan presents of himself: the gender inequalities noted by Wood proliferate into issues of social class. Such common folk are incapable of comprehending the work of a great artist like Isa (or Ceylan). As before, the effect is not to disparage the intelligence of common folk, but to self-deprecate.

It is no coincidence that Ceylan, like Isa, relies heavily on contemplative scenes of landscapes in his films. This is not to say that Ceylan nihilistically – as Bülent Diken regards his films (2008) – gestures to the pretensions of beautiful scenery. Rather, by highlighting his pomposity of character, Ceylan produces a contradiction that radically challenges the authority of the artist's stylistic decisions and its incomprehensibility to an untrained eye. He implicates himself in a self-deprecating scenario, disrupting his authority, forming a dialogical pathway with the spectator who is implicated in the disentanglement of this contradiction. Ceylan self-deprecates to traverse either side of the partition between creative genius and spectatorial ignorance.

FRAGMENTATION

Continuing analysis of the rearrangement of aesthetic partitions, this second point regards the fragmentation of the *mise en scène*. I shall broach two apparently separate forms of fragmentation in the film. The first regards the fragmenting of the face from its surroundings in a close-up. Unlike conventional facial close-ups, these faces are devoid of any discernible meaning or motive. The second regards the montage of irrelevant images. During a sex scene, we are shown places deliberately removed from the sexual act. Furthering this aesthetic of equality, Ceylan's fragmentations show what is usually not shown, drawing attention to elements which, whilst present during it, do not normally have an active role in the screened action. Each fragmentation is a disassembling and reassembling of a recognisable distribution of the sensible. As I will demonstrate throughout these two points, fragmentation disrupts convention and expectation and, in turn, invites the spectator to engage.

Theories of fragmentation in art are usually connected to theories of modernity. This is especially prevalent in younger art forms, like cinema, invented as it was at a time of revolutionary technological and social change. In the early twentieth century, political theories regarding the malaise and crises brought about by the fragmentation of society and of the self were broached most influentially by liberal sociologists like Max Weber and Emile Durkheim. Walter Benjamin turned to the Baudelairian *flâneur* figure in his *Arcades Project* (1999), which sought both to explain the fragmentation of urban modernity, while also incorporating fragmentation into his writing's formal presentation. City symphony films of the early twentieth century were also engaged in this formal elaboration of fragmented experience, using abstracted modes of vision to reorient the spectator's relationship with built environments. The close relationship between film (as montage, which is an essentially fragmented mode of representation) and the fragment is, therefore, evident from its origins. In turn, due to these early debates on the fracturing of previously coherent, unified forms of community prior to rapidly developing industrialisation (that would become today's global capitalism), forms of fragmentation in art are frequently attached to these commonplace sociological theses. Such tendencies are especially common in postmodern theories of art. For example, fragmentation is one important element of what Fredric Jameson called 'the cultural logic of late capitalism' (1991). Jameson echoed this symbolic view of fragmentation in his discussion of Vincent Van Gogh's shockingly bright portraits of peasant life:

> [T]he willed and violent transformation of a drab peasant object world into the most glorious materialization of pure colour in oil paint is to be seen as a Utopian gesture, an act of compensation which ends up producing a whole new Utopian realm of the senses, or at least of that supreme sense – sight, the visual, the eye – which it now reconstitutes for us as a semiautonomous space in its own right, a part of some new division of labour in the body of capital, some new fragmentation of the emergent sensorium which replicates the specialisations and divisions of capitalist life at the same time that it seeks in precisely such fragmentation a desperate Utopian compensation for them. (Jameson 1991: 7)

For Jameson, a fracturing of the social fabric is reconstituted in Van Gogh's style in a very direct way: an entirely novel sensory response to the emerging social conditions is defined as a fragmentation of the sensorium. A direct line from social change to artistic form is hereby envisaged by Jameson and followed through in his revisionary response to modernist art. This comes to inform a new, postmodern form of 'psychic fragmentation' (ibid.: 398). All earlier, coherent, totalising frameworks for explaining how one experiences the world are thrown into disrepute. Postmodern art practice comes to utilise this fragmentation of sensory experience in the late twentieth century. By positing the fragmentation of social and psychic experience in the twentieth century, Jameson is following the likes of Durkheim, Weber and Benjamin before him. However, his lucid elaboration of postmodernism is significant and unique, because it coins a way of understanding a whole era of art and aesthetic experience in ways entirely determined by the new division of labour brought about by the historical and social realities of global capitalism. How might we relate these notions of social and aesthetic fragmentation to the fragmentation of *Climates*, when we analyse the film outside of its immediate socio-historical sense and instead in a politico-aesthetic sense? In turn, how might we subvert Ceylan's own 'unpolitical' position and shed light on *Climates*' egalitarian approach to spectatorship? I shall claim that fragmentation becomes a political aesthetic mode not with a sociologically symbolic function, but as a way of responding to spatial hierarchies that are carried over from the hierarchies of spectatorship into the space of the image. Deconstructing and reconstructing the cinematic image offers a way of exciting the spectator's response and levelling this hierarchy of spectatorship. This occurs, first, most notably, through the fragmenting of the face from the body.

Due to its popularity in silent film, the close-up was of great interest to early film theorists. Hugo Münsterberg submitted an early but still relevant thesis on the psychology of the close-up, claiming that 'the mind concentrates itself on a special detail in its act of attention; and in the close-up of the moving pictures this inner state is objectified' (Münsterberg 2002: 110). Münsterberg's approach is so accurate it appears unarguable: what else is the close-up if not a simulation of our own concentration? Contemporary film theory often follows this path too. David Bordwell and Kristin Thompson define the close-up in this purely formal manner, describing its function according to distance (2010: 262) or as a motif through repetition (ibid.: 264). In a similar sense, Richard Maltby discusses close-ups in empirical terms in order to discuss the evolution of a classical approach to cinematography (Maltby 2003: 333). What these approaches show is a disinclination to probe the poetry of close-up images and to explore how their effects are quite often at odds with what they purport to tell the spectator. In *Climates*, we regularly find ourselves confronted with opaque close-ups, due either to their expressive blankness or to their lack of psychological import. There is a political dimension to this kind of fragmenting of the face from the rest of the body. To do so acknowledges its presence and activity in a social environment, which in this case is the environment of the surrounding *mise en scène*. When we consider the quite majestic landscapes in *Climates*, closing in on a tightly framed image of a face makes a bold statement about what is being excluded as well as what is being shown.

In the film's introductory sequence, we see Isa photographing ancient ruins in a desert landscape. Throughout the sequence, we are shown extreme close-ups of Bahar's face in extended duration (Figure 4.1). To focus so insistently on the face (rather than the object of her husband's attention) is to demonstrate an equality of importance: this face is as important as those

Figure 4.1 *Climates*: the face of Bahar is shown in close-up for extended periods in the opening sequence.

majestic landscapes. Isolating the face in this manner asks us to contemplate the character's experience over the event itself. Bahar rests her head against the white stone of an ancient ruin, her eyes half closed, gazing downwards. The shot is divided into a split-screen: her head and shoulders on one side and the eroded stone on the other. The sunlight shines on her face as she tilts her head away to gaze towards the left of the screen. The cut shows several pillars, from behind which Isa appears, taking photos. Cut back to Bahar: she looks on, then away again, yawning and leaning back against the stone. When she walks over to Isa, they hold each other in a half-hearted embrace, seemingly content in each other's company. Bahar wanders from the ruins, into the background, towards the surrounding fields. Isa is now shown in close-up, absorbed in his photography. The next shot shows Bahar walking towards the screen, from the top of a hill. She stands at a height down from which she can view Isa. Another shot/reverse-shot sees her smile at Isa tripping over. Her expression, again in close-up, goes from smiling to sadness. All in close-up: her lips part, her breathing heightens, a tear falls from her face, her eyes then shift from where Isa is to somewhere unknown. A piano is heard, then the title appears.

The mystery and opacity of Bahar's expression (particularly in the final image) is demanding because it forces us to imagine the unseen. It is, in this sense, an invitation to what Béla Balázs called a 'strange new dimension of the soul' (Balázs 2004: 316). Balázs's writing is vital for our understanding of how the face is capable of acting in isolation from the other elements in the frame. In his important writing on the close-up, he paraphrases Marx:

> 'The root of all art is man.' When the film close-up strips the veil of our imperceptiveness and insensitivity from the hidden little things and shows us the face of objects, it still shows us man . . . The close-ups of the film are the creative instruments of this mighty visual anthropomorphism. (Balázs 2004: 316)

The 'anthropomorphism' of a film (the film's capacity for dialogue with the spectator) contains the potential for an aesthetic redistribution. The play of facial gesture (which Balázs refers to as 'microphysiognomy' [2004: 319]) confounds the spectator and alludes to something unknowable and unassignable. It forces contemplation of something unseen and yet referable, seen and indefinable. Balázs called this 'a new world' (ibid.): something transcendent beyond what the image might otherwise portray. However, perceiving this 'new world' has always been a possibility for the spectator. In *Way Down East* (D. W. Griffith, 1920), the film to which Balázs is referring, a 'new world' is implied through Lillian Gish's gestural gymnastics. One particular moment in Griffith's film involves the same formal redistribution of aesthetic partitions that occurs in Ceylan's film: the face exists in the frame for longer, the gestures are less definable and more far-reaching, and the surroundings are forced into the background. By incorporating Ceylan's close-ups into an egalitarian model of spectatorship, I am following Mary Ann Doane in her claim:

> [T]he embrace of the close-up . . . is an attempt to salvage spectatorial space, to reaffirm its existence and its relevance in the face of the closed, seamless space of the film . . . this celebration of the close-up is also an attempt to reassert the corporeality of the classically disembodied spectator. (Doane 2003: 98)

Doane's reference to 'the disembodied spectator' raises two elements of interest to this argument. First, it claims that, by bringing the spectator into closer dialogue with a human subject, there is some attempt to envelop the spectator into the film for empowering (rather than pacifying) purposes. On the one hand, this reinforces my point on certain aesthetic tendencies initiating Ceylan's reconfiguration of the hierarchy of spectatorship. On another, however, the corporeality of the close-up references the camera's closeness to the actor's body and the subsequent feeling of intimacy and involvement for a spectator. Thus, as well as figuratively re-embodying the disembodied spectator through what Balázs called a 'strange new dimension', Ceylan's close-ups also bring the spectator closer to the physicality of the actor. Again, opacity is a key factor here. Rather than simply providing access to something clearer than ever before, heightening proximity to opacity brings us closer to something we cannot understand.

The second form of fragmentation follows this logic – an instance both corporeal and indiscernible. As with the opaque facial close-ups, the sex scene's montage of irrelevant objects similarly fragments with the aim of incorporating the spectator. This is the second sex scene in the film and since it differs so completely in form and content from the first, it is certainly intended to work comparatively. While the two do not appear so coldly and divisively analytical in this very subtle film, I contrast them since their differences are so enlightening with regards to the overarching aesthetics and politics of equality in the film.

The first sex scene occurs shortly after Isa and Bahar break up. It involves Isa and Serap (a former fling). The sex in this scene is awkwardly played, voyeuristically framed and arguably non-consensual. The intensity of the violence involved is heightened through the distanced long take: Serap is shoved across the floor from his thrusts until they both exit the frame. This distanced long take presents a marked contrast to the close-up long-takes usually employed throughout, recalling the unbearable rape scene in *Irreversible* (Gaspar Noé, 2002) or the manipulation of Elena in *À ma Soeur!* (Catherine Breillat, 2001). Excepting those films' overt thematic concern with sexual violence, all three films share a distanced perspective of sex. These moments tie down the spectator in a corner of the event's space through an impairment of vision and force us to endure an intolerable act. Again, reminiscent of *Funny Games*, there is a question to be asked about the way this scene contributes to debates on the ethics of spectatorship. As Catherine Wheatley explains, the 'moral problem centres on the spectator's realisation of themselves as a scopophilic subject' (Wheatley 2009: 106). However, unlike Haneke's use of visual impairment,[6] Ceylan is not depriving his spectator of information; we know what occurs beyond the frame. The second sex scene between Isa and Bahar contrasts in its presentation of the corporeal dimension.

The scene plays out quietly and delicately, denying speech and determinedly limiting access to psychological rationalisation of acts, movements and gestures. Whereas the earlier scene was a depiction of what we may argue constitutes non-consensual sex, this scene is arguably not even sex. The night before he is scheduled to leave the country and return to the city, Isa is shown in his hotel room. Bahar appears at his door and enters without a word. She lies on the bed and he sits beside her before resting his head on her ankles. In silence, we cut to a close-up of her face, then her hair. There is a shot of his hand in her hair, his face buried in her hair, a close-up of her eye. Then to the back of her head in the bottom half of the screen, with the top-half of his face in the top-half of the screen (Figure 4.2). These are the images that precede sex or happen alongside it, flirting with the idea of the sexual act without directly showing the action itself. By fragmenting the parts of the act which usually go unseen from the earlier scene's vulgarity, it makes sense to attach the shallow relationship of Isa and Serap with one kind of representation, and to attach the spiritual

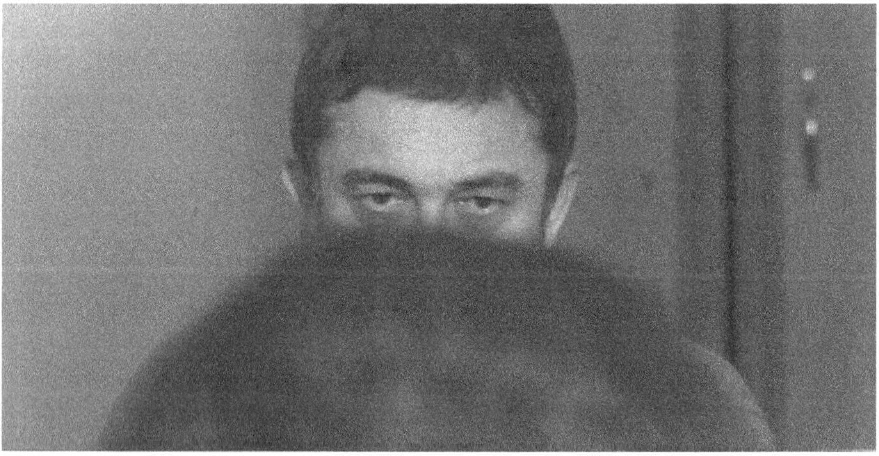

Figure 4.2 *Climates*: focusing attention on objects and body parts usually deemed less significant in the presentation of sex, a poetic approach is produced that continues Ceylan's use of visual fragmentation as a mode of equality.

relationship of Isa and Bahar with this latter one. Ceylan is not engaging in the kind of moralising about the complicity of spectators that we arguably find in the work of Haneke, Noé or Breillat – he is inviting a reconsideration of how we perceive moving images of sex. In the first, we see a darkly self-conscious version of the pornographic: Serap's top is torn, she is immobilised by Isa, the man dominates, the affect is somewhere between hysterical, offensive and embarrassing. It is a direct depiction of sex, entirely unpoetic. With little room for interpretation beyond the further self-deprecation of Ceylan's character, it demonstrates how not to engage a spectator. The second is the opposite: indirect, beautiful, the graceful chimes on the soundtrack heightening the sense of poetry. To be clear, it is not that Ceylan places gentle carnality above rough sex. Rather, he contrasts literality with suggestiveness through representations of two different kinds of sex, to oppose the clear directorial import of the former with the poetic free-play of the latter.

The fragmentation of close-up images that do not appear directly related and exceed the conventional representation of sex perform the same function as that signalled in the facial close-up: as claimed by Doane, this is an attempt to 'reassert of the corporeality of the classically disembodied spectator' (2003: 98). As before with the opaque facial close-ups, Ceylan recasts the spectator's perception and role in the film. Fragmentation reconfigures the arrangement of elements involved in the depiction of sex, substituting pornographic displays with the flicker of an eye, the overlap of limbs and the smothering of hair. The supposedly irrelevant images enact equality by casting light on the unseen, prefiguring the visibility of a spectator.

SPRING

My final point regards the film's delineation between what has and has not really happened in the narrative reality of the diegesis. Ceylan's situating of himself within the film works to soften the boundaries between the profilmic and the extra-cinematic. Rancière has written extensively the constructedness of realities. As discussed in Chapter 2, the discursive formation of the past through a poetics of knowledge recognises that reality itself is an unstable category. While Rancière introduces this concept through the realm of historiography and the documenting of 'truth', it reappears in his writing on art and literature through the notion of 'fiction'.

> The real is always a matter of construction, a matter of 'fiction' . . . What characterizes the mainstream fiction of the police order is that it passes itself off as the real, that it feigns to draw a clear-cut line between what belongs to the self-evidence of the real and what belongs to the field

> of appearances, representations, opinions, and utopias. (Rancière 2010: 148)

What passes for reality or non-fiction is no more than discursively formed configurations and perceptions. These configurations extend into the popular consciousness, creating normative assumptions, sculpting facts and lies into dichotomies of the real and the unreal. Ceylan's traversing of diegetic and non-diegetic spaces is a testing of this binary. I refer in this final point to moments that stand out for the ambiguousness of their actuality: moments that force the spectator to question the level of reality she has just seen. By creating such an effect, *Climates* gestures towards another enactment of equality: between two sorts of knowledge and recognition of its poetics. The scenes suggestive of fantasy are useful here.

This sequence occurs immediately after the dinner party scene broached at the outset. A ground-level close-up taken from the top of Bahar's head captures her sunbathing on a beach – the lush blue sky and bright sunshine fills much of the screen. A cut then shows a low-angle silhouette of Isa, muttering something indistinct down to her. The next shot shows Isa strangling Bahar, ploughing her head into the sand beneath her. Cutting then to Bahar awakening, Isa lies beside her and tells her that they need to talk. Out of the dream, the two of them are indeed at the beach. Isa explains that he is leaving her, stating that he is too boring and old for her. She clearly does not buy his excuse, as she sits silently. We then see them leaving the beach on Isa's motorcycle, Bahar forced to hold onto Isa's torso in what must be the most awkward of return journeys. Bahar is shown in close-up: the backdrop blurs, her face is an image of disorientation. She covers Isa's eyes from behind as they ride, sending him into a panic, veering the bike off-road crashing to the ground. This is, figuratively, *unreal* – unprecedented for the narrative thus far. Without the prior dream sequence, one might judge this moment as an extreme shift of Bahar's character, mitigated (albeit only slightly – she did almost kill them both, after all) by their break-up. Bahar walks away, leaving Isa with his bike. In the next scene, Bahar sits on a coach alone, before Isa boards. The crash is not mentioned, but Bahar has a plaster on her hand: does this mean it really happened? The extremity of the event, in conjunction with the prior scene, produces an ambiguity between what is real and what is fantasy.

In its disruption of the fiction's illusion of reality, the softening of the boundary between reality and fantasy is perhaps the most drastic act to perform in fictional narrative; but it also explicitly relates to Ceylan's project in general. Following the discernible difference between Bahar's dream and awakening at the beach, the possibility that what we see is merely dreamed is a constant that is never definitively signalled. This collapsing of reality and fantasy has radical ramifications for the rest of the film: how are we to judge what has happened so far and what is to come? What is happening for real and what is happening only in the imagination of the individual? The site of this ambiguity is a vital point and only one figure emits it. Only Bahar poses the challenge. Isa is a 'realist', to pessimistic extents; dreams have very little part to play in his life. It is Bahar who confounds the spectator's comprehension. In the opening sequence, in her dream at the beach, through the expressive performance of her mental escape throughout conversations, Bahar always appears quietly pensive and deep in contemplation. She is often present only in body: she dares to dream.

However, through this duality, the film could be viewed to simply rehash the classical stereotype of women as essentially enigmatic. A strong similarity is drawn here with the films of Michelangelo Antonioni, with whom Ceylan shares a great deal aesthetically and thematically. Writing on *L'Avventura,* Luciana Bohne critiques the film's attempt to frame Monica Vitti's protagonist as a subjective agent. The slow gaze at the contemplative woman becomes 'yet another signal of the threat she poses as a real woman, since her disproportionately lengthy time on camera . . . succeeds, instead, in . . . exposing her to the audience's look – a look that is compelled to fetishize her' (Bohne 1984: 21). Does Bahar perform the same conflicted function as Vitti in her iconic performances of women in crisis? By repeating the style of modernist auteurs before him, like Antonioni, Ceylan runs the risk of attracting their earlier criticisms. However, while the performance, experience and visual constructions of Bahar's pensiveness and alienation are remarkably similar to Antonioni's films of the 1960s, the suggestion of mere fetishisation of appearance is undermined when we consider Bahar as emblematic of the broader destabilisation of cinematic hierarchies. When we conceive of *Climates* as a role-traversing, quasi-autobiographical film, Bahar is more than a woman just subject to the gaze; she personifies diegetically a disruption to Ceylan's privileged role. Bahar's dreaming is an attempt to redistribute the sensible within the profilmic space, staging the equality that may follow in the extra-cinematic realm through the attachment of the spectator to the other in Ceylan's own life.

Bahar has a second, significant dream later in the film. She recounts it to Isa following the second sex scene, explaining that she was soaring over a meadow, towards a cemetery, where she could see her mother who had come back to life. The romantic inference of this dream is obvious: she clearly feels settled having reconciled her relationship with Isa. When Isa responds with nil interest and reminds her of her imminent departure for work, she simply smiles. In this moment, she finally recognises the absence of Isa's absolute inability to dream and his imprisonment in one, rigid, configuration of reality. On the one hand, this continues the deprecation of Isa's character, but it also underlines Bahar's significance. It is only Bahar who is capable of connecting and of loving, since only she places faith in the unseen. Bahar – Turkish for 'spring', which is the only season not depicted in the film – signals new life, unknown formations of what we know and can imagine. In the film's final image, the dreamer has left Isa. As she works on her film set, her body fades from view, disintegrating into the air, leaving only the blue sky and falling snow in the frame. The spectator is left with this image of transience between materiality and spirit, between real and fantasy, between the fiction of the film she is producing and the reality of her personal life. In this final scene, all three elements of Ceylan's equality come together: the self-reflexivity of a 'performing' performer, fragmentation – first of her opaque expression, then of the blank sky – and the equivocation of fantasy and reality. The final dissolve is a literal disintegration of Bahar (and her symbolism of 'the new') into thin air. *Climates* gestures towards a reality yet to come: hope for 'spring' is shown as latent within the present configuration of reality.

Triggered by the initial traversing of inside and outside of the diegesis, the aesthetic procedures of *Climates* rely upon the spectator's engagement. This is something other than testimony that 'the effect of [the artist's] idiom cannot be anticipated' (Rancière 2009c: 22). These words from *The Emancipated Spectator* would appear to preclude any necessity of interaction with Ceylan's particular motivations with regard to his spectator. Instead, my claim hinges upon the action whereby the authority figure steps down from the seat of power, arm extended, holding out an olive branch. Recognising the continuing importance of the auteur to film studies, my point is not to disregard the genial artist altogether in the way Barthes did and countless others do today. Rather, through the highly personal *Climates*, Ceylan offers an idea of the filmmaker as a subject with genial powers, only to undermine the pedestal upon which those powers are said to be enacted. The author is not dead; nor is he supreme, unique, immortal or omniscient; he is equal to the spectator. Ceylan gestures to the figure who most threatens his subjectivity, the birth of whom supposedly occurs through his death: the spectator.

Despite what Ceylan describes as *Climate*'s 'unpolitical' character then, I claim that it provides a space that is acutely political. These questions on authorship, spectatorship and aesthetics are necessary ones. As Barthes recognised, by shifting attention to reception, the possibility of plurality is developed over and against the singularity of a privileged perspective. We learn through Rancière that the denial of equality is not permanent – or even 'real' – it is merely a partition. Ceylan demonstrates the superficiality of this divide through his traversal. The banality of the facial gesture, the visual properties hidden during representation, the imagined over the actual: Ceylan develops this abstract plurality of subjectivity into an aesthetic approach. These filmmakers who feel most compelled to repel an association with politics: perhaps it is they who should be analysed most carefully from a political aesthetic perspective. The likes of Ceylan and those I have mentioned in relation (such as Tarkovsky, Antonioni, Breillat, Noé, Haneke) are auteurs who consistently reject the label of politics, yet consistently invoke political consideration.

What has become of politics to make it such a dirty word, to make it worthy of such contempt by filmmakers like Ceylan? If it is true that the consensual nature of twenty-first-century neoliberalism is to blame, then the anti-political filmmaker may offer an alternative: a way out of the mire of contemporary political discourse. Hidden within the claims of an 'unpolitical' film is a kernel of optimism – decipherable without recourse to the terms of state politics: Bahar's promise of, and faith in, the new.

NOTES

1. He addresses this opinion in an interview that is included on the Artificial Eye DVD release of *Climates*.
2. In this sense, this discussion of the hierarchies of spectatorship would seem to mirror some of the critique of Althusser undertaken in *Althusser's Lesson*.
3. While Conley is engaging with Rancière's writing, he introduces a level of originality to the analysis that really distinguishes his approach his from Rancière's.
4. In the case of the former, Bülent Diken views the film as simply an embodiment of Turkey's contemporary in-between geopolitical and cultural status (2008). Gönül Dönmez-Colin uses the film as an example of the increasingly progressive engagement with gender politics from contemporary Turkish filmmakers. Both frame the film as, very much, significant for *national cinema* debates (2008: 166). In the case of the latter, Julia Banks mentions Ceylan's self-reflexive employment of the photographer character (2010). Kristi McKim broaches the film's deployment of seasonal change as a way of questioning 'the iconography of cinematic seasons' for similarly self-conscious purposes (2013: 178).
5. This scene is mentioned in almost every review I have read of the film, in Wood's article and in Dyer's *Zona* (2012). The commentaries always celebrate Ceylan's honesty and incisive cultural critique.
6. For instance, the desperate mother crawling to her murdered child in *Funny Games*, the Baron's closing of the door behind him upon news of Archduke Ferdinand's death in *The White Ribbon* (2009), or multiple moments in, and perhaps the entire premise of, *Hidden* (2005).

PART III

Between Politics and Cinema

CHAPTER 5

Akomfrah's Foreigner

> [T]he foreigner . . . persists in the curiosity of his gaze, displaces his angle of vision, reworks the first way of putting together words and images, undoes the certainties of place, and thereby reawakens the power present in each of us to become a foreigner on the map of places and paths generally known as reality.
>
> (Rancière 2003: 3)

In his short text, *Short Voyages to the Land of the People* (2003), Jacques Rancière uses Roberto Rossellini's *Europe '51* (1952) to present an early thesis on representations of politics in cinema.[1] The 'curious gaze' of Ingrid Bergman's grieving, foreign, bourgeois housewife escapes the social distribution of the post-war Italian class system, transforming the spectator's known field of vision. As well as Rossellini's film, *Short Voyages to the Land of the People* uses the foreigner figure to address the transformative potential the poetry of Wordsworth, Rilke and the utopian socialist philosophy of the Saint Simonians. These diverse encounters frame the foreigner as something other than the pitiful outsider from today's news coverage. Instead, the transformative potential of foreigners comes to realign the partitions distinguishing one reality from another; the figure embodies a unique political potential, capable of instigating radical social reconfiguration. There is also something significant about Rancière's collation of various art forms. While the thematic concern for displacement and reconfiguration remains, the foreigner migrates across forms, invoking an aesthetic strategy alongside the social one. Taking up Rancière's explicit concern for the foreigner's gaze alongside his implicit disregard for medium-specific analysis, this chapter utilises the political aesthetic potential of the foreigner to further my exploration of the politics of art cinema. Recognising Rancière's foreigner as a figure that is as effective formally as much as it is thematically, the foreigner disrupts the politico-aesthetic as much as the socio-historical realm. The concept thereby produces a rupture in the neat divide I have thus far installed between a cinema of politics and a politics of cinema. The foreigner in art cinema lodges us *between* cinema and politics, providing strategies for society in its artistic invention and for art in its social analysis.

Like Rancière's other inquiries on film and politics, *Short Voyages to the Land of the People* uses cinema in a solely illustrative way. The suggestive, poetic style of his prose uses the visual and written texts as examples of how politics might be imagined outside of the existing totalising paradigms. I would like to push Rancière's observations further, broaching the foreigner as a pivotal figure for occupying the gap between a cinema of politics (the representation of social configurations) and a politics of cinema (the reconfiguration of aesthetic experience). As I explained in my introduction, art films contain a political potential when they address a people, not with the intention of exclusively reinforcing an 'us' that already exists but of inclusively insisting upon its expansion. By occupying the interval between cinema and politics, the foreigner activates and excavates spaces for a people in a political aesthetic sense. To elaborate, I turn to the intermedial explorations of foreignness in the work of John Akomfrah. Working across several forms, Akomfrah engages with migration technologically, institutionally and thematically, to provide an important perspective on the political potential of art cinema. Through analysis of his essay film *The Nine Muses* (2010), I wish to claim that the foreigner is a construction both political and aesthetic, occurring through the redistribution of sensory partitions relating to art and literature as much as the history of migration.

The Nine Muses broaches the theme of historical migration to Britain. It is the product of myriad images, sounds, writings, arranged into a film that seeks to render formally and thematically the experience and subjectivity of the migrant figure. Akomfrah appropriates passages from Homer's *Odyssey* to comment on the idea of mythmaking by referencing the original mythmaker, thus locating an origin fable for the foreigner. Using Odysseus's experience of being foreign, Akomfrah leans on *The Odyssey*'s status at the beginnings of the literary canon to reconfigure the partitions framing our understanding of the migrant experience. A redistribution of the sensible occurs, altering the meaning we attribute to these classical narratives. At the same time, the disruption to this narrative is achieved through the production of a peculiar formal approach. Through the correlations drawn between images, sounds and text, the cinematic construction of the foreigner imagines a spectatorial foreignness through its interlinking of multiple media forms. Akomfrah has been working across different media since his early work with Black Audio Film Collective in the 1980s, utilising tape-slides, television and docu-fictions made for the cinema. In the twenty-first century, Akomfrah's work has taken on a notably familiar route: he produces video installations for galleries before often editing the material in the form of essay films that screen in the more conventional arthouse cinema. I shall first turn to the 'gallery film' (Fowler 2004) as a mode that fragments the art cinema experience and reconfigures the spectator's relationship with the film. The material conditions of these installations redistribute the sensible in physical as well as contextual, thematic, aesthetic and formal ways.

THE POLITICS OF THE GALLERY FILM

With a status close to art cinema, the gallery film emerged in the 1960s and has since been conceived as occupying the similarly fraught space between elitist spectatorship and critical engagement. The form now has a rich history of political commitment. In his far-reaching assessment of the field, *A History of Experimental Film and Video* (1999), Al Rees relates such commitments to European avant-garde filmmakers of the 1920s. The likes of Eisenstein, Walter Ruttmann and Hans Richter were forced, ethically and industrially, to negotiate two extreme ideological poles, combining formal experimentation with social observation. Richter would come to term this approach constitutive of a 'social imperative' (Rees 1999: 53) for film. The manifesto culture of this era laid the groundwork for an alternative form of cinema: one at odds with conventional practices of production, distribution and exhibition. Rees applies this counter-cinematic tendency to discern a key difference between art cinema and artists' cinema.[2] This counter-cinematic tendency evolves in the avant-garde filmmaking that arises in the United States during the 1960s. Many of the key filmmakers exhibiting work in the gallery at this time are often grouped under the banner, *structural film*. In P. Adams Sitney's seminal *Visionary Film: The American Avant-Garde 1943–2000*, structural film was said to have broken from the poetic tradition of lyrical film in 1920s Europe by prioritising form over and above content (Sitney 1974: 327). By sidelining the thematic and foregrounding formal play, structural filmmakers such as Michael Snow and Kenneth Anger were clearly concerned with questions of spectatorship, such as: what is the relationship between spectator and moving image? What does the film want from us? What are we to do after viewing? Broaching Sitney's claims on the structural film's formal minimalism, R. Bruce Elder (2006) claims that the structural turn encourages 'apperceptive activities' that create a distance between film and spectator that 'makes them aware that the work confronts them as an object' (Elder 2006: 125).

One of the foremost structural filmmakers, Paul Sharits, was a clear proponent of this principle. Sharits was concerned with using spatial and temporal apperception to politicise the gallery film experience, attaching the gallery's subversive use of extensive duration to the manifestation of 'democratic ideals' (Sharits 1978: 80). Steven Jacobs has taken a similarly utopian view of the gallery film, claiming that this new form of spectatorship promotes 'the emergence of a new spectator and a new spatialisation of the moving image' (Jacobs 2011: 152). In its reorientation of spectatorship through challenges to several aspects of film production and exhibition, the gallery film offers surely one of the foremost political versions of art cinema. However, there is a sense of déjà vu in the association of politics to a preferred artistic mode, in ways very reminiscent of political modernist theory. As Kate Mondloch explains, such a mode of address 'runs the risk of demanding a predetermined and even compulsory response' (2010: 26). This sort of response, of course, runs parallel to the kinds of representational social narratives people like Sharits were vehemently opposed to. We can, therefore, see how some perspectives on the gallery film quickly repeat the critical tendency to conform to the stultifying logic of political modernism's 'embodied allegories of inequality' (Rancière 2009c: 12).

While much writing on the gallery film repeats the earlier flawed coupling of a critically engaged, distanced spectator with political potential, I do not believe the gallery film itself must be understood as stultifying. Rather, if we engage with the distance incurred for the spectator as properly *open*, the gap created by distance need not be conceived as simply awaiting the placement of a preferred intellectual argument. It is in this sense that I would like to consider the gallery film's importance as a space of *betweenness*. Filmmakers working between the gallery and the cinema are regularly preoccupied with the political aesthetic project of redistributing a sensible arrangement of forms and spaces. As Alison Butler has argued:

> Gallery film and video installation is a hybrid form, situated between the institutions of cinema and the art gallery and anticipating new media practices. It registers its historical location between media forms and institutions in the intricacy and multiplicity of its spatial and temporal dynamics. While this deictic uncertainty may be seen as contributing to the dislocated condition of viewers, it can also be used in subtle and precise ways to address the complex situation of the contemporary subject in mediatized time and space. (Butler 2010: 323)

Butler describes the gallery film's essential challenge to predefined spaces for each art form. In its betweenness, there is something apparently disruptive in works like Akomfrah's that unsettle our idea of art, or cinema, or politics, which responds in a disruptive way to the contemporary experience of consensus. Disrupting the unified cinema space (which produces a spatial wholeness for the spectator to take up an allotted position), gallery films provide an interruptive exhibition space, often employing multiple entry-points and exit-points that never close, undetermined lighting conditions and a greater diversity of seating and screening positions. This in turn produces a less predictable response from the spectator. To be clear, I do not mean to suggest that the gallery film's disruptive environment obstructs cinema's ideological construction of the spectator's subjectivity in the vein of Jean-Louis Baudry's Lacanian critique of cinema (1974). As I have demonstrated in the previous chapter, art films are sometimes concerned with democratising the relationship between film and spectator within the confines of the cinema in ways that need not 'reveal the mechanism' (Baudry 1974: 46). The distance invoked by gallery filmmakers can, in this sense, be broached less as a matter of *verfremdung* and more in terms of fragmentation: not of the image but of the viewing space. Using aesthetic principles employed in the diegesis of some art films (deriving from the same bourgeois forms derided by political modernists like Baudry) and employing them at the level of exhibition, gallery films often fragment the sensible order of the cinema – a unity of sound, vision, time and space – and displace the spectator's angle of vision in ways resonant with the experience of foreignness.

This chapter explores how this works in *The Nine Muses* through three key points. First, I build on Rancière's definition of the foreigner through a close analysis of the scenes involving the West Indian man (as he refers to himself). These scenes, I claim, are a process of constructing a profile for the foreigner in two senses: through the poetic characterisation that draws upon a multitude of figures (from both classical 'high art' and popular 'low art' texts), but also through the man's side-on facial close-up – a pictorial profile – which invokes an affective response from the spectator, haunting us long after the film has finished. From this initial point, I move on to engage with the method by which Akomfrah pieces together his film. His fragmenting of texts produces a foreign aesthetic: displacing the angle of vision and reworking their function. Fragmentation is hereby shown to be a natural continuation of his gallery installations – the fragmenting of cinema's unity of sound, vision, and space into the hybridised, montage form of the essay film. Taking this point further and focusing on one specific form of image, my third point addresses one of the film's particularly salient artistic techniques, derived from another art form: the use of tableaux. The tableau is a traditional staging technique that becomes revitalised in *The Nine Muses*, appropriated in the form of digitised portraiture, contrasting starkly with the film's use of archive footage (which appears damaged and old-fashioned by comparison). Akomfrah's foreigner is subjectified through an asynchronous relationship to the history of art. Like Homer's verse, forms from the past are shown to provide insight into new subjects, reawakening the power present in each of us to become a foreigner.

PROFILE OF A FOREIGNER

We see a shipwreck, tinted brown, as though the image itself has aged and was found moored up on some foreign shore. Mozart's *Adagio* plays as the camera pans across the rust of the wreckage before holding on the ripples of water that move slowly towards us. The piano soundtrack is simple and slow, using mainly high notes that evoke a sober scene of recollection. A calmness is formed, but as though something significant, perhaps awful, has just occurred. There is cut to a canted shot of the boat lopsided in the water, its sail aloft beside it. Then another cut to a man, smoking, gazing out through his window. A voice is heard, describing 'the terror' of the solitude felt in 'the West Indian's arriving' in Britain. Shortly after this, we are shown footage of this audible man being interviewed. Agreeing with the pictured interviewer's question ('And then you get settled?'), the man replies, 'you get settled and then you, too, become part of the strangeness'. These images – the way they are framed and adjusted, the musical and visual accompaniments played out through the montage – all coalesce to construct what we might describe as a profile of a foreigner. I use this term to evoke the political aesthetic techniques at work, here. On the one hand, an attempt is made to construct a representation of the foreign subject, universalising this experience in ways that ironically subvert the practice of 'racial profiling'.[3] On the other hand, the profile is a formal approach to framing the image – side-on, in close-up (Figure 5.1). This first point addresses this dual form of the profile.

The cut from the shipwreck and voiceover takes us to a new person; another

Figure 5.1 *The Nine Muses*: a close-up of the West Indian man is shown in profile, as his account of migration is read in voiceover.

foreigner, this time, is shown smartly dressed, on his way to work. This image is framed by what we have just heard (here is another West Indian who feels the terror of isolation) and continues to be framed by what we hear now ('however tough he is, for the first time he is alone'). After the clip of the interview, we see lines from a Mesopotamian poem about journeys. After this, we hear more classical music: Handel's 'Care Selve' performed by black soprano Leontyne Price. These disparate elements continue to build upon the West Indian man's description, as does the next, anonymous, dark-skinned man, first shown sitting beside his newlywed wife. A record player is foregrounded in the frame giving the impression that 'Care Selve' is playing in their living room. We then see this second man in close-up, thoughtfully looking out towards the edge of the frame. This is followed by a voiceover passage from Homer's *Odyssey* in which Odysseus describes to his mother his maltreatment by his hosts. This voiceover takes us to the end of the scene. We see images of the second man taking the bus to work and archive footage of a third man, working at a factory. All three are embodiments of the words uttered by the first foreigner whose short description of the foreign experience is multiplied by networks of disconnected sounds and images. Akomfrah is building upon the West Indian man's description of one's acclimatisation into strangeness. He pieces these disparate elements together to articulate the aesthetic experience of strangeness.

As if to draw a conclusion from this montage, the image of a silent man follows immediately the profile of a West Indian man. His calm silence embodies the foreigner's representational paradox: historically enormous but officially invisible. This finds its clearest expression when we return to the West Indian man. We do not hear him speak again; we only see him – his face shot in close-up profile, gazing off-screen. A suturing reverse-shot shows him watching a record player, echoing visually the record player in the newlywed couple's sequence. This time we hear Paul Robeson: not an operatic performer, but, like Price, a black singer whose training differs from the historically acknowledged black tones of gospel, blues or jazz. Robeson's voice – deep, refined and stately – is entirely distinct from the history of popular black music in the West. One could be forgiven for mistaking his singing of 'Let my people go' (itself an ancient document of migration, referring to Moses's defence of the Jewish people in the Book of Exodus) for theatre. Robeson, though, was a committed thinker, activist, traveller and pursuer of his cause. Blacklisted during the McCarthy trials due to previous socialist activities, his signifying status (a black Hollywood performer who left a profound mark during his time in the spotlight) is vital. The West Indian man studies the vinyl as the song plays, as though the lyrics were written on its surface. Listening to Robeson sing about the gathering of a tormented people, this image conjures an impassioned idea about historical struggle and unity across time and borders. This man becomes an exemplary 'foreigner', standing for all else we see and hear in *The Nine Muses*.

Yet, there is something missing from the above which cannot be accounted for through the film's gathering of sources into a profile. There is something singularly startling about the West Indian man's first appearance that arrives in the cut from the calm, post-shipwreck sea to his brooding presence at the window. He haunts the film, returning later, without voiceover announcement. This haunting, affective dimension has no obvious rationale – there is no common sense behind his persistence in the spectator's thoughts nor in the return of his image later in the film. This figure's haunting quality is the result of another profile: the side-on image of the face. Caught watching, portrayed askance, hiding a suggestive inner depth, the close-up profile of the face of the foreigner intensifies the figure's pensive gazing. This haunting quality is the result of the connection established between image and spectator, which, in this case, is testament to the communicative potential of the foreigner. As such, we might connect this to the moment of 'reawakening of a power present in us' (Rancière 2003: 3). What is so haunting about this image? We might consider it in terms of Rancière's description of 'political art' and the necessity of something uncanny (Rancière 2004: 63) – something which, in Freud's terms (to whom Rancière is surely alluding),[4] departs from common aesthetic categories of beauty and pleasure and produces instead something unsettling. Rancière referred to Irene in *Europe '51* to argue that experiences that are at once suggestive and disruptive of political signification provide an exemplary space for politics, through

> a radical uncanniness that threatens to destroy all political meaning . . . It undoes the sensible fabric – a given order of relations between meanings and the visible – and establishes other networks of the sensible, which can possibly corroborate the action undertaken by political subjects to reconfigure what are given to be facts. (Rancière 2004: 63–4)

As I have argued elsewhere (Harvey-Davitt 2014), Rancière's writing on *Europe '51* is some of the most engaging, poetic and productive analyses he has produced on cinema. However, the implications of his definition of 'political art' are such that film can be no more than merely suited to the evocation of politics. The film's formal strangeness disorients the spectator and forces the spectator to reconsider the social arrangements made available to them, in post-war Europe. Taking further his observations on the uncanny effect of cinema and politics, we can raise the stakes here: if a film is capable of corroborating the reconfiguration of a social experience, we can no more have a political cinema than we can a *cinematic politics.* Thus, when the uncanny disruption of political signification and aesthetic innovation clashes in this manner – when a collision occurs between the challenges to both epistemes – it no longer makes sense to isolate the event to a solely artistic or social experience: we are seamlessly caught between cinema and politics. This is precisely the space Akomfrah has sought to occupy with *The Nine Muses*. The haunting image of the West Indian man interrupts the neat configuration of scenes, sounds and texts that plot the construction of a foreign profile. This happens for several reasons which all occur at once: the shift from an exterior to interior environment, the change in colour, in image quality (from digital to film stock), in the speed of the image and the notable manipulation of frame rate to produce a slow-motion effect. These are comparative differences produced through montage, which go some way to explaining its effect; but there are also elements in the image itself, the significance of which do not depend on its relation to the cut, but through the *mise en scène*'s inherently haunting quality. There are ghostly elements at play here: the play of light and dark from the sunlight on his body; his shadow against the wall lining up behind him; the smoke from his cigarette creeping unnaturally through the slow motion; the faint reflection of something unknown in the windowpane, as though superimposed on the houses outside. In this four second scene sandwiched between the contemplative images of a shipwreck, the ghostly qualities of the smoking man at the window 'undoes the sensible fabric' (Rancière 2004: 60). As we will soon see, it is he who speaks in the background and explains the foreign experience with such clarity. Layered upon images of boats, the sea and a foreigner in his new home, the voiceover surely paints an evocative picture; but that moment of the man at the window undoes all of this.

This is confirmed when he reappears, surprisingly, twenty minutes later. We see children tossing planks of wood and debris into a bonfire, then a cut to a group of black police officers striking a white man with a baton before tossing him into the back of a van, then a cut takes us to a close-up of the West Indian man's face. At the cut, we also hear words from Book I of Milton's *Paradise Lost*: 'What in me is dark, illumine. What is low, raise and support.' As these lines are read, the unusual activity of his eyes – furiously blinking and darting back and forth – suggest intense and possibly vengeful thinking. Unlike his first scenes, the camera's new proximity to his face builds on the heightened tone of the images before and after it, evoking our alignment with what appears. As he looks to the edge of the frame it is as though he views what we view, thereby adjoining his ambivalent expression to the prior images of destruction and violence. Both this second image and a third (which follows shortly after) of the man thinking, appear to offset, and become offset by, the scenes of fire. The juxtaposition of the pensive face and images of destruction seem at once to question the validity of violence, but also to test the calmness and intellect of the man. In the face of physical antagonism, the man is shown to provide a less documented alternative: he wonders how to act in the face of the strangeness he earlier described. This is repeated when we see him for a third time. Wood is burning, producing the sound of embers and flames crackling as the camera zooms in. A cut then takes us to an extreme close-up of the man, gazing off-screen. However, unlike the visual confinement of the earlier image, this cut opens out onto the space around him, showing objects in his room – including a record player. As he listens to the words of Robeson, we do not simply match the West Indian man with the activist, whose cause is similar. As he bows his head onto his knuckle and watches the record spin, we see a man in deep thought about how to respond to a situation, listening to the words in order to learn how better to protest injustice. This image conveys a sense of his frustration and depth of thought.

The West Indian man's profile exists in-between the descriptive analysis of the migrant in postcolonial British society and the haunting affect of bodies in an image; between the sociological montage of words, sounds and images and the sensory disruption of those elements that provokes a response from a spectator. He is the meeting point for all Akomfrah's other disparate elements, allowing us to make sense of things; but he also embodies just how fleeting and disruptive of the 'common sense' the foreigner figure essentially is. This is the way of things in *The Nine Muses*: constantly shuttling back and forth between the discernible and the indiscernible, the socio-historical and the politico-aesthetic. 'Undoing the certainties of place', this thwarting of sense underlines, at once, the political potential of the foreigner to cinema and his cinematic potential to politics.

FRAGMENTATION AND BETWEENNESS

The profile of a foreigner in the guise of the West Indian man is constructed through a method of fragmentation: fragments from a multitude of literary, musical and visual texts are connected, with the effect of developing both an identity for the unidentifiable migrant and an aesthetic that is sufficient for the foreigner. In the previous chapter, I explained how Ceylan uses fragmentation in ways that cannot be explained through either modern or postmodern theories of sociological symbolism; rather, in *Climates,* fragmentation is used to respond to spatial hierarchies carried over from the hierarchies of spectatorship into the visual composition of the image. This shift from the socio-historical to the politico-aesthetic characterises both Ceylan's and Kaufman's politics of cinema – each, I claimed, determinedly constructs a political redistribution through the cinematic without necessary recourse to a sociological context. In the case of *The Nine Muses,* however, the sociological dimension cannot be underplayed. That is, for Akomfrah, the essayistic montage of disparate texts and art forms is the mode that best embodies the foreigner's undoing of the certainties of place. Migrating between media, foregrounding textual overlaps, fragments are contextually determined by the social and cultural experience of the foreigners of world history. However, since Akomfrah is keen to show the breadth and apparent timelessness of the foreigner's experience, this fragmentation also does not constitute a cinema of politics (in the vein of Panahi's long takes or Larraín's use of obsolete technologies). Deriving no more from a determined social situation than from a generic aesthetic framework, the fragmentary aesthetic of the foreigner must be understood as something between politics and aesthetics. I shall demonstrate how this betweenness involves a dialogue between the gallery film and the art film.

Although fraught with difficulties and existing hierarchies, the gallery space provides political possibilities for film. To understand the development of Akomfrah's approach, we need to consider the textual fragmentation of *The Nine Muses* in line with his other, non-cinema works, in order to rehearse briefly a method that recurs in the films of artists working between gallery and cinema. We must view Akomfrah's method of working between the gallery and cinema as both constitutive of a fragmentary aesthetic and constituted by the subject of foreignness. Fragmentation is also a symptom of the gallery film's fragmenting of the unified spatio-temporality of the cinema space into an unsealed site of fluid temporality. When video work is exhibited in a gallery setting, the relationship between screen and spectator is itself fragmented, exploding the wholeness and ambience of the cinema to a freer site, permitting movement and discussion. When exhibited in the gallery, cinema becomes fragmented in two senses. First, it undergoes a physical fragmentation: images, once ordered through montage, are often placed beside one another on multiple screens, recalling the traditional, pre-cinematic *framing* of images in a gallery setting. Sound is also often derived from alternative sources, asynchronous to the film itself. Most notable, however, is how the conventionally communal relationship of an audience is fragmented into individuals, wandering in and out of the gallery space. Secondly, invoked by this first point, we are returned to the pre-democratic era of images producing a metaphysical fragmentation: the gallery's grip on the *aura* (which Benjamin celebrated the decline of with cinema) seems to return. Thus, in turn, there looms the threat upon the democracy of spectatorship: films return to the gallery as a kind of nostalgic longing for artistic *quality*, removed from the sight of the plebs.

It is probably fair to distinguish Akomfrah's motivations from this second point: from *Handsworth Songs* onwards, his films are models of democratic engagement, totally devoted to people that have been deprived of a voice in official histories. In Akomfrah's gallery films, like the Rancièrian foreigner figure, fragmentation displaces one's angle of vision and reworks the way images are put together. Taking up the historical (d)evolution of images to and from the institutional setting, it is as though Akomfrah appropriates the dissolution of the communitarian site of the cinema and reconstructs a democratic space for the foreigner from the fragments left over. The profile of the West Indian man and its liquidation of cultural, historical and aesthetic boundaries embodies this transition from gallery to cinema. His dual profile performs the disruptive sensory experience of the gallery film. In what follows, I shall interrogate the points of intersection between fragments in *The Nine Muses* to consider further how the foreigner's disorienting, fragmenting gaze connects Akomfrah's gallery film aesthetic to his art film montage.

In the film's opening sequence, we hear an angelic howl atop some dissonant guitar strings. Images of an anonymous snowy hillside are pictured. We are about to see something epic. We then see the first piece of text:

> The gold fell very high in the sky
> And so when it hit the earth
> it went down very deep.

Set against the industrial sounds of thumping steel drums and the impeccably captured, picturesque mountaintops,[5] this sentence reads like a recitation of the actions of Zeus. The words come from the testimony of a migrant worker, as documented by eminent art critic and theorist John Berger in *A Seventh Man* (Berger and Mohr 1975). In this opening minute, we have an expositional scene providing the technique for the rest of the film: fragments of new visual footage, diverse music and poetic intertitles, developing the thematic concern with the foreigner. By rearranging these words (from their original place in Berger's prose into a poetic stanza), Akomfrah also introduces another of the film's tropes that is achieved through the fragmentation of multiple sources: the realigning of a social status. As with the West Indian man's egalitarian embodying of multiple sources from high art and popular culture, this introductory sequence produces a similarly democratic trajectory (from Greek myth, through Berger's writings, up to the found audio testimony of migrants) with its dramatic tone and aesthetic reordering of words. A cut takes us from a boat sailing past these snowy mountains to archive footage of an anonymous black man (the archetypal migrant figure of Akomfrah's films) working in a factory, staring blankly downwards as he turns the cogs of the apparatus. This is the first time we see the film's socio-historical subject as human being and, therefore, the first time he is situated amongst these disparate threads of Greek mythology and aesthetic theory. We zoom in on his face and hear the aural testament of another migrant, whose words deplore the unjust persecution of foreigners. This brief depiction of the sights and sounds of post-war British migrant testimony fades to another intertitle, explaining (in a couple of sentences) the plot of Homer's myth before quickly returning to the mountains. We then gain more intimate access to the face of the mountain, as a slow pan scrolls up the rocky facade. The next cut takes us to archive footage of a snowy day on Birmingham's roads, suturing the two wintry scenes. This juxtaposition produces an important point that echoes throughout: a Greek epic has unfolded in recent British history that is now carved into our landscape.

The primary literary source soon shifts from Homer to Milton's *Paradise Lost* – a passage from which is heard, overlapping scenes of a snowy day in a British suburb. Relating again a classical text that is loosely based on the tragedies of migration (this passage describing Eve's transgression and banishment from Eden), the idea of something world-historical unfolding in Middle England recurs. Try as we might to attach the words of Milton to the images sourced by Akomfrah, it is difficult to see the rationale behind the descent from paradise in the snow-covered suburbs of England. These are quite banal images set against a quite magnificent story, which is itself the point here: not symbolic of the matching of sound and image, but demonstrative of the idea that the epics of Homer and Milton have occurred in these banal spaces, but in a very muted, hidden way. A voice for the migrant (from the postcolonial West Indian to the present-day target of the EU) seems minimal but is historically and culturally monumental. These literary references are thematically related, but historically undetermined, thus demonstrating their continuing relevance. As we find throughout, the literary references range from the classical era, the Enlightenment, up to more recent prose by the likes of Samuel Beckett. As we jump back and forth from these quiet English suburbs to the glacial landscapes, all the while hearing the prose of great writers, we are enlightened about the persecution of the foreigner.

All the other fragments of Akomfrah's film will cross similar, glacial landscapes. Its image recurs, evoking a sense of awe, obstacle and tragedy. These are the physical landscapes that have been crossed by foreigners, but they are also representative of the labour of struggle and necessity of grit that these people must undertake. Beyond what they represent, we can also consider the response elicited from the spectator upon viewing these juxtapositions. At various times, they invoke a feeling of barrenness, alienation, vulnerability, as though we are in the middle of nowhere in the most unforgiving of climates. Coupled with the minimal testimony we have heard so far (on the injustice of the foreigner's persecution), this mood makes sense in this context; but it also generates a sense of general alienation on the part of the spectator. Just like the aesthetic profile of the West Indian man and its antagonising with the social profile of the foreigner, the landscapes of these wintry tableaux themselves incur a slight disjuncture with the sum portrait of the film's fragments. What should we make of this contradiction, drawing upon isolation to construct a space for collectivity? To offer some answers and by way of conclusion, I shall turn to some words written by Rancière in relation to Campement Urbain's *Je et Nous* (2003–8). This collective art project situated on the outskirts of Paris shares with *The Nine Muses* a desire to engage with disparaged communities through the experience of solitude. In turn, it also shares a contradictory impulse, at odds with the empathetic aims of the implied themes (understanding and experiencing foreignness), setting solitude against community. For Rancière, this contradiction is essential:

> Aesthetic experience has a political effect to the extent that the loss of destination that it presupposes disturbs the way in which bodies fit their functions and destinations. What it produces is no rhetoric persuasion about what has to be done. Nor is it the framing of a collective body. It is a multiplication of connections and disconnections that reframe the relation between bodies, the world where they live and the way in which they are 'equipped' for fitting it. It is a multiplicity of folds and gaps in the fabric of common experience that change the cartography of the perceptible, the thinkable and the feasible. As such, it allows for new modes of political construction of common objects and new possibilities of collective enunciation. Now this political effect operates under the condition of an original disjunction, of an original effect, which is the suspension of any straight cause-effect relationship. (Rancière 2009c: 72–3)

Across different texts, Rancière's argument on the 'condition of an original disjunction' echoes the 'radical uncanniness' (Rancière 2004: 63) mentioned earlier: between *Short Voyages to the Land of the People*, *The Politics of Aesthetics* and *The Emancipated Spectator*, we find a repeated invocation to realise our inner foreigner. Akomfrah's fragmentation attempts the same. He pieces together hybrid fragments of foreign texts to evoke a sense of foreignness for the spectator. The intertextual relationship between the different glacial landscapes, across texts from within and outside the canon, extends this, situating politics in a space of betweenness. *The Nine Muses* does not just illustrate the link between aesthetics and politics – the film *becomes* the site of politics, constituting both a political aesthetic disruption in the present and a space for a people to come.

DIGITAL TABLEAU IMAGES

Fragmentation incurs disruptive moments throughout the film. One key fragment is the tableau of glacial landscapes. The tableau image essentially upturns technological hierarchies in the arts. Literally translated as 'living pictures', the political aesthetic significance of tableaux in *The Nine Muses* is significant in two senses. First, the form's ontological connection between life and art implies a productive network between the living picture of this fictional foreigner, the lived experience of an actual foreigner and the foreign spectator to come. Second, as a form that cuts across the arts – from classical portraiture, to theatre, right up to its contemporary popularity in contemporary audio-visual installations – the tableau is also between media. The effect of mixing old techniques with new technologies is shown to initiate a multisensory experience, embedding the political potential of the foreigner in the aesthetic choices of *The Nine Muses*. Let us revisit what must have been the initial motivation for *The Nine Muses*. It is an attempt to transplant the mechanisms of recent British history – the story of post-war migrants re-settling – onto ancient mythology. As such, the film both questions the certainties of place peculiar to the foreigner and the progress made by historiography's evolution from chronicling histories. This in many ways echoes Larraín's approach in *No*. Historical narratives can be told in multiple ways – by utilising diverse techniques, *The Nine Muses* provides unseen perspectives, perhaps soothing historical wounds and potentialising a foreign subject yet to come. That Greek mythology so profoundly prefigures and demarcates a way of understanding more recent migrant narratives initiates several subsequent formal decisions taken by Akomfrah. The film mixes old and new forms to examine the breadth of possibilities available through the historical discourse of art film techniques and technologies.

Brigitte Peucker has described the use of tableaux in film as offering 'a moment of intensified intermediality' (Peucker 2007: 26). Existing between media would seem to fuse neatly with Rancière's declared distaste for medium specificity (McNamara and Ross 2007: 85). By indiscriminately utilising old and new techniques, and using old and new technologies to reframe them, *The Nine Muses* stages the shift from the regime Rancière described as 'representative' into the 'aesthetic'. Narratives and images break free from the stranglehold of classicists and art historians. Formal determinism is relinquished, so ideas can more freely indulge in the appropriation of techniques from various art forms. The obliteration of categorical disciplines is an affront to disciplines that have historically excluded the marginalised from self-representation in art. As I mentioned in my introduction, Rancière has made a similar claim on *Colossal Youth*, in which the slum-based worker, Ventura, is refused entry to the gallery (Rancière 2014b: 132). *Colossal Youth* reconfigures the gallery space in the service of the excluded. This, in turn, redistributes the access and representation in the arts more equally. However, the foreignness of *The Nine Muses*' intermediality breaches the conventional narrative form of art cinema, situating this redistribution in a space of betweenness. From the initial redistribution of the mythological narrative, Akomfrah realigns the partitions categorising those that warrant mythologisation. This fundamental intention can be found in specific figures (like the West Indian man), in

Figure 5.2 *The Nine Muses*: one of several spectacular tableau images, staging the journey of the foreigner in a timeless manner.

specific spaces (the glacial landscapes) but also in specific techniques like the digital tableaux.

The tableaux that occur in *The Nine Muses* are the only original images the film contains. All other images derive from the archive. In one tableau, we see an anonymous figure standing before some vast, white mountains (Figure 5.2). During the sequence profiling the West Indian man, overlapping the aural monologue of Odysseus's maltreatment, this anonymous figure is shown standing on the edge of a cliff that overlooks docks and stormy skies. A slow zoom seamlessly centres our gaze and – when combined with the image's stillness and the alarm on the soundtrack – unsettles us. The voiceover declares, 'they [the perpetrators of his maltreatment] brought me here', situating this anonymous figure at the scene of a crime. There are other moments, detached from voiceover, which are equally striking. A white aeroplane – almost camouflaged amidst the pale blue sky and white mountains – sits eerily isolated, before a cut to archival footage of RAF personnel removing the protective covering from a commercial jet. In the archive footage, passengers board an airplane; in the tableau, the plane is remote, viewed from afar by two anonymous, bright-coated figures. This tableau offers two points of interest. First, there is the indiscriminate approach to art historical boundaries of technique and technologies; but there is also a second effect, produced through the content of the image, the stillness of the camera and the slowness of the zoom. The strangeness of these elements is made even more apparent when placed against the fragments of archival material. Distinct from the onslaught of archival footage – so dynamic and astute in its depiction of the migrant experience – the tableaux in *The Nine Muses* are unsettling. They demand our attention on a quite empty image. Yet, if empty, from where does this unsettling uncanniness derive?

Peucker claims this uncanniness is an essential feature of the cinematic tableaux, produced through its liminal location between art forms: 'Film is a medium in which different representational systems may collide . . . suggesting that those moments in films that evoke tableaux vivants are moments especially focused on film's heterogeneity' (Peucker 2007: 31). By using an archaic form, the heterogeneity of cinema apparently becomes pronounced. Since heterogeneity is crucial to both Peucker's argument and to my own approach to the political potential of art cinema, the incorporation of earlier forms would seem to provide an especial portal to politics. This is a little too simplistic, though. For Rancière, film's heterogeneity is simply a continuation of principles first established in German Romanticism, such as Kant's subjective universalism, Lessing's *Laocoon* or Schiller's 'aesthetic education'. The Romantics promoted a radical equality between subject matter, form and quality of perception. Read in line with the tableaux in Akomfrah's film, we can measure the difference between Rancière's romantic model and Peucker's preferred version of filmic reality. For the romantics, all art forms are capable of expressing reality equally effectively. For Peucker, the tableau image introduces 'the real into the image' to such an extent that it 'collapses the distance between signifier and signified' (Peucker 2007: 31). By challenging the association of a preferred form with the experience of reality, we might, in turn, come to question the political aesthetic implications of Peucker's argument: do tableaux provide an especially productive way of critiquing and redressing a social, political reality?

While Peucker's view of the tableau image as realigning the partitions delineating the hierarchy of sensory responses to an image (from *seeing* to *feeling* a scene) is relevant and useful for my purposes, her approach to 'the real' and its essential attachment to heterogeneity privileges a specific mode in ways at odds with what I have argued thus far. Cinema is art, tableau is a technique: neither are preferential forms of representing anything. By privileging 'the multimedial' or 'the intermedial' text as in some way superior to other approaches, a hierarchy of heterogeneity is established that could be seen to hierarchise the 'best' formal approaches for achieving political art. I have tried to argue that Akomfrah's films exist in a state of betweenness not to prioritise the gallery film, or montage, as political forms, but instead to highlight the social and historical weight of the foreigner as a strategic figure for both politics and cinema. It is not that Akomfrah's foreigner offers a more viable political aesthetic strategy than Panahi's disagreement or Ceylan's equality. Each is rather an attempt to redistribute its own social arrangement: Panahi's state decree, Ceylan's spectatorship, Akomfrah's migrant subject.

While we cannot generalise the tableau image's ability to redress political realities more effectively, we can nevertheless question the sum of Akomfrah's combining digital tableaux and its arresting results on the spectator. Two quite contradictory things occur in these moments. We are first presented with the political statement that all people can be the subject of classical, painterly art: a migrant or, more properly, an anonymous figure is pictured here. However, while this straightforward socio-political argument is no doubt made palpable throughout the film, it cannot account for the arresting effect incurred. They do not feel *more real* than the documents gathered from the past; nor do they evoke a greater sense of reality than the sound of Robeson matched to the tortured expression of the West Indian man. However, they do produce a similarly haunting effect, but in a very different way. Distinct from the immersiveness of the West Indian's close-up, these landscapes numb us. In direct contrast to Peucker's claim on the positive possibilities of the tableau, I would in fact claim that Akomfrah produces an *anaesthetic* quality with these tableau images. It appears all has ceased, that history has paused, that we now exist in a time after the action of migration and rioting and all that is left is a void: an image of consensus. Unlike the haunting quality of old, forgotten images profiling the lives of acclimatising foreigners, these immaculate portraits of glacial landscapes arrest us only in their mundaneness, estranging us from the humanity exhibited throughout the fragments. The significance of this technique lies, I believe, in Akomfrah's foreign take on technologies: he skews both the affirmative and cynical arguments on the changing formats of cinema. Just as the digital camera of Ceylan's *Climates* prospers most effectively when it freezes the image and returns us to a pre-digital era, or as Larraín finds political significance in obsolete technologies, Akomfrah undoes the privileged certainty of digital's clarity without damning it altogether.

While the rest of the film's fragments are masterfully reworked and juxtaposed to heighten the foreign experience, the coldness (both glacial and alienating) of these digital tableau images works to offset the emotive capacity of the archive. We might similarly compare the fecundity of the speech of the common foreigner in the film with the Homeric base; or the interchangeability of the words of Berger and Mohr's anonymous foreigner with the characterisation of a Greek god. A horizon is drawn amongst the broken fragments of old and new, which are then reconfigured in a foreign way.

The foreigner dominates social discourse today. By reconsidering the political aesthetic possibilities of foreignness, *The Nine Muses* challenges the known ways of being and doing and raises the political stakes of art cinema in consensual times.

NOTES

1. The original French version was written in 1990 – five years prior to *La Mesentente* (Rancière 1999) and ten years prior to the original French publication, in 2000, of *The Politics of Aesthetics.*
2. Or what Richard Abel terms 'the narrative avant-garde' (Abel 1987).
3. A discriminatory process historically performed by police powers to determine the character traits of ethnic minorities.
4. While Rancière's fondness for the writing of Schelling – who gave an earlier account of the uncanny – is pronounced in a number of his works, the Freudian uncanny is the most famous and is of aesthetic interest throughout Rancière's *oeuvre* (see for instance, *The Aesthetic Unconscious* [2009b]).
5. Which, consequently, are Alaskan, but certainly resemble British landscapes like Snowdonia or the Lake District in winter.

Conclusion: Contemporary Political Art Cinema

Do art films offer more than a mere illustration of some abstract theoretical notions? It will no doubt be hard to convince those with a preference for hard, empirical realities that anything but (at best) a political discussion or portrayal is happening in these films. While I have sought to critique Rancière's own view of cinema as representational only, I have also argued that his political aesthetic theories offer a way of locating politics in and through film. However, Peter Hallward has more roundly criticised Rancière's theories, claiming that the association of politics with aesthetics 'encourages us to do little more than "play at" politics or equality' (Hallward 2006b: 128–9). Does Rancière's political theory leave a potential for simply giving up and accepting the way things are? This sentiment is broached directly by Yves Citton:

> We, people of the 21st century – aware of all the traps and past failures of political agency, calls to arms and other glorious revolutionary projects (so the postmodern story goes . . .) – we like it whenever someone suggests that we can be 'subversive' by simply sitting there with our eyes open: our hands are unlikely to find themselves covered with blood in the process, we are unlikely to be hurt or jeopardize our (after all fairly comfortable) conditions of living. (Citton 2009: 121)

One should clarify this passage; Citton actually goes on to complicate such a simplistic view of things. Yet, in presenting this perspective in the first place, he articulates an important point that could be levelled at Rancière's work – and certainly my own: *how are films – even the most innovative and committed films – worthy of the rare label Rancière names 'politics'?* To claim that politics occurs in and through one of these films goes further even than Rancière's *use* of films for theorising the political. I shall use this conclusion to summarise why I think the answer is 'yes' and to bring together some final thoughts on contemporary political art cinema.

Let us first revisit some important points on the redistributive activity of politics. As I stated in the introduction, Rancière defines politics as the redistribution of the partitions framing a social order, meaning that bodies assigned to one role attain the capacity for escaping that location and taking on another one. These partitions exist in every social order – every environment that hosts interaction between living beings. When I claim that political activity is potentialised in each of these films then, I am claiming that the social distribution constructed in advance of a viewing experience is *reconstructed* after viewing. Moreover, when I claim that 'a cinema of politics' and 'a politics of cinema' exists, in each case, I am claiming that the dual social environments of the diegetic world of the film and the social reality of the spectator is mutually engaged in political activity. Indeed, it is the shared distribution of the sensible constructed in each film experience (not just Iranian censorship laws or Panahi's film itself, but the amalgamation of all these elements through our watching of *This is Not a Film*) that works to delimit and *re*limit the parts and positions of each social order.

Let us begin with Panahi's film then. After *This is Not a Film* was released and acclaimed near universally by critics, the Panahi case gained a fair level of international coverage, heightening public awareness of the artistic persecution of those in theocratic authoritarian regimes. Panahi went on to make *Closed Curtain* (2013): a poetic, meta-fictional story of an artist confronted with the realities of the world outside when a couple of rebels hide out at his sanctuary in a barren corner outside Tehran. In 2015, he won the top prize at the Berlinale for his quasi-documentary *Taxi* (2015), in which he is disguised a cab driver, using the tense union of private/public in the space of a cab journey to goad passengers into divulging the contemporary realities of Iranian city life. We may argue that none of these subsequent achievements were possible without *This is Not a Film.* Had this video diary not reached its illicit destination, demonstrating the thirst for dissent from those around the world, would Panahi have continued? Either way, the instigation for further action is (like this whole project) immeasurable. *This is Not a Film* departs from the conventional way of making political films. It shows the spectator the banal, lived experience of a 'political prisoner' and constantly attempts to foreground discussion of the creation of art over discussion of social prohibition. It works according to the principle of Rancièrian disagreement: not opposition to what the government says, but, rather, contention over what speaking means. Since Panahi disputes not so much 'the right to speak' but the speaking situation in general, he snatches the reins from those who decide what is and is not speaking – or filmmaking – in general. Thus, because everything about Panahi's film (its premise, its content, its thematic (un)concern, its manner of address) hinges upon this act of disagreement, we can see that this is something other than a documentary *about* politics: this is the coming-into-being of a political agent and the blueprint for a political art cinema.

This disagreement also comes to inform a radical version of art cinema's stylistic heterogeneity. However, the kind of stylistic heterogeneity produced by Panahi's multitude of aesthetic disagreements cannot be contained by Bordwell's description of art cinema, defined 'explicitly against the classical mode' (Bordwell 2002: 94). Despite the diversity of noted stylistic elements, Bordwell's definition does not sufficiently account for the series of aesthetic disagreements of *This is Not a Film*. It covers many factors, including Panahi's opposition to 'defined desires and goals' (ibid.: 96); his interest in reaction over action (ibid.); the overt signification of social forces; the focalising of the author in the film's system (ibid.: 97); and the frequent spectatorial impulse, 'when in doubt read for maximum ambiguity' (ibid.: 99). However, if Panahi's work is constitutive of art cinema (as opposed to its other possible discursive categories of, say, documentary, or Iranian cinema),[1] we require a broader frame of analysis than Bordwell's. Galt and Schoonover's location of impurity throughout aesthetic, historical and industrial modes of analysis results in the idea that art cinema 'always perverts the standard categories' (Galt and Schoonover 2010: 6). This presents a very clear link between the mode of politics envisioned by Panahi (his subtle 'efforts' to pervert the available, standard categories) and a shared characteristic of art cinema in general. As such, the political potential of art cinema is always built on an imperative to pervert standardised categories.

While Panahi's antagonism with the ontology of both politics and cinema presents an especially appropriate discussion of Rancièrian politics, Larraín's is perceivable only when we recognise the function of ambivalence that pervades the film. History, for Rancière, is grounded in the ambivalent location between science and art: caught between the empirical trace of an event and one's subjective experience of it. *No* foregrounds the 'poetics of knowledge' in the official history of dictatorship in Chile through the film's self-reflexive redistribution. The ambivalence of René thwarts the politics of left and right: he suffers in a dictatorship, but he also becomes the spanner in the works of the leftist, humanitarian narratives of representation for the Chilean people. *No* challenges the empiricism of what we see through its provocative aesthetic, which redistributes three sensible orders: the function of 'the star', the obsoleteness of old technologies and the visual flaws that occur therein. Such self-reflexivity is an essential component of art cinema, prominent in many of the theories discussed thus far. Bordwell refers to such moments as 'authorial marks' (Bordwell 2002: 100), defining such thoughtful creative novelty as merely tepid formalism. Indeed, the contemporary result of such 'marks' – far from sites of ambivalence from which to instigate the redistribution of an aesthetic hierarchy – names one of the most common traits of a commodified, socially disengaged version of art film, which Russell J. A. Kilbourn describes as 'postmodern parodic art cinema characterised by radical self-reflexivity and ironic distanciation' (Kilbourn 2013: 102). Between these two nihilistic versions, however, there remains the possibility of reclaiming a form of self-reflexivity for the purposes of historical insight. Were it not for its self-reflexive marks, *No*'s commentary on the transition to democracy might read very differently. As it is, an ambivalence arises out of the tension between the formulaic narrative template and its subtle punctures of irony, producing uncanny images that appeal to an alternative response. Neither propaganda for the regime nor revising the visibility of the disappeared, the self-reflexivity of *No* follows Rancière's Michelet by 'making them speak as a silent people' (Rancière 1994: 45).

The critical function performed by these aesthetic disruptions works to multiply the trace of the disappearance, surrounding *No* like a topic made taboo twice over: first in its literal covering by authorities, second in its impossibility of representation. *No*'s ambivalence thus challenges an ethics of representation that deems some issues unrepresentable. As such, it potentialises the political subjectification for the spectre of a disappeared people, without covering or pretending to embody their historical invisibility. In *No*, we find a redistribution of the partisan laws of party politics as well as of the sensible order that attaches representation to visibility and silencing to invisibility. A pervasive, spectral presence haunts the film's images through which the silenced come to speak as a silent people. The dual function of representation alludes here to the aesthetic paradigms of politics and the realignment of the sensible order governing how historical narratives should be represented. *No*'s ability to signal debates on unrepresentability through the low resolution of video technologies, or the utilisation of light through a camera's lens flare, demonstrates the potential for political activity arising out from the formal elements alone: what I have called 'a politics of cinema'. It is in this sense that I have argued that politics might occur even in avowedly unpolitical works.

My first analysis of this sort focused on Charlie Kaufman's *Synecdoche, New York*: a film whose postmodern polemics on the impossibility of action apparently snuffs out any sort of political relevance. The protagonist's obsession with creating a masterpiece leads to the construction of pure simulacra, clearly mimicking Baudrillard's writings. *Synecdoche* appears to present something akin to Fukuyama's 'end of history' – the idea that, irrespective of our most inventive attempts at novelty, the state of things is unalterable. However, a challenge appears through the film's aesthetics. Through the editing of sound and images beyond the comprehension of the protagonist, Caden embodies the possibility of change through his sped-up perception alone. His vision for an alternative within the world – his performance of 'dissensus' – confronts the anaesthetising rhythms of contemporary America. When he chooses the most confined of locations from which to plant the seeds of this dissensus, the creations that grow from within demonstrate the possibility of reconfiguring existing social orders. *Synecdoche, New York* is a film that stages political activity through the intensification of one's experience of time and space. Political subjectivity is potentialised purely through techniques unique to cinema: intensified editing and figurative *mise en scène*.

However, the film's containment of political activity within the satirical mode limits art cinema's political potential. Unlike Panahi's disagreement with the policing of cinema and the Iranian state, or Larraín's antagonism with the options available to Chilean voters, the dissensus of *Synecdoche* occurs in a solely diegetic manner: two worlds in one, never to transgress the fictional world of the film. This constriction surely tends to affect art cinema in general. Bordwell opposes art film to the primary political form of the era: what he calls the 'historical-materialist order of cinema' (Bordwell 2002: 101), which refers to the films of Godard, Straub and Huillet, Kluge and Farocki to name a few. What distinguishes these filmmakers from art filmmakers (his key references are Dreyer, Antonioni and Bergman) is their use of Brechtian principles of distanciation 'to analyse art film assumptions about the unity of ideology' (Bordwell 2002: 102). This reflects the view of Comolli and Narboni: '"bourgeois realism" and the whole conservative box of tricks', as they described it (Comolli and Narboni 1971: 5). Yet, unlike the *Cahiers* writers, Bordwell pulls those who might have been placed in 'category c' – 'criticism practiced through form' (ibid.: 6) – into the fold. For Bordwell, art cinema becomes the apolitical alternative to Hollywood.

While there is a sense of this in *Synecdoche*'s 'domestication of modernism' (Bordwell 2002: 102), since it is so vehemently resistant to conventional formal strategies of time and space, it is clearly something other than bourgeois realism. Moreover, attached to its formal deconstruction is a quite scathing dissection of a multitude of American cultural hypocrisies, antagonising further the idea that art cinema is blind to ideology. Thus, what is revealed by approaching a stylistically audacious, socially aware, but politically limiting film like *Synecdoche* is the near impossibility of understanding contemporary art cinema in a socially *unaware* manner. Perhaps this was always the case. Maybe it was always short-sighted to relegate the humanist films of modernist cinema to the margins of political aesthetic analysis. To make stylistically heterogeneous cinema that reflects and engages with the contemporary is to always propose an insight into the ideological symptoms of its culture, and, in turn, to allow for a kind of social consciousness. The extent of this social consciousness will of course vary. More concretely, we might claim that the criticality of art cinema – in fact, of all cinema – has been significantly shaped by political modernism of the 1970s, by theories of identity in the 1980s and by the continuing theoretical experiments taking place in the nexus between continental philosophy and the moving image. Despite the limits of films and theories that solely speak *about* ideology (rather than affecting a more palpable change), this *aboutness* (as New Historicists termed it)[2] forced a near ubiquitous appreciation for the omniscience of social forces. So, while there is a clear divide between social consciousness and actual, felt, political action, another important divide exists between social consciousness and so-called bourgeois realism.

In Chapter 4, I argued that Nuri Bilge Ceylan's *Climates* shares Kaufman's overt concern for framing the possibility of politics within postmodern debates. Instead of the death of the author, what we instead find in *Climates* is an attempt to intensify the role of the author to masochistic extents. Ceylan acknowledges his unjust position at the head of a hierarchy and seeks to dismantle it from within, redistributing several sensible orders: the mastery of the artist's intellect is thwarted through ironic self-deprecation, the unity of the image is disrupted through the fragmentation of bodies, and the partition between reality and fiction is softened through narrative ambiguity. While Ceylan himself has come to distance his narratives from political metaphors (imagined between his films and Turkey's ambivalent relationship with Europe),[3] his masochistic performance and testing of boundaries throughout *Climates* can be seen to initiate equality – the fundamental principle for the possibility of any political interruption, for Rancière.

Like Kaufman, the philosophical themes of Ceylan's films complicate the clarity of their political relevance. From his early works, up to *Winter Sleep* (2014), the socio-political context of consensus politics is barely detectable. This is a filmmaker clearly concerned first, foremost, perhaps solely, in questions of *humanity*.[4] Again, mirroring Kaufman, existential torment fuels these narratives and *Climates* is certainly a part of this tradition. However, the political activity of *Climates* does not rely upon a representation of political themes or events; the egalitarianism of the film shows itself in the images: the image of an ignorant Ceylan facing off against the nuanced expressions of his wife; the fragmentation of the image into its lesser seen quarters; the indiscriminate interweaving of fantasies and realities. Ceylan's timeless, humanist stories contain an aesthetic novelty that is concerned with undermining the notion of authorial superiority. This is a way of making art at the expense of the artist's authority, without destroying altogether the conceptual existence of artists. Implicit in this approach is a series of questions carving out Ceylan's political aesthetics of equality: what role do we play? How do we recognise our privilege over others? How do we counteract it? This is a severely self-reflexive mode of production that raises important political questions despite its apparently unpolitical character.

Yet, in its humanistic character, is *Climates* capable of affecting change outside of the world of the film? Is it more akin to Kaufman's social consciousness within the film alone? Do we simply experience a staging of equality, tantamount to Hallward's argument? While we cannot locate specific real-world changes that attach *Climates* to a clear political strategy, the difficulty of superimposing existing social antagonisms on its narrative differs from the clearer themes of *Synecdoche*. Kaufman's film stages, then thwarts, a familiar postmodern cliché on Western society, but the political aesthetics of *Climates* produces more subtle territory, demanding engagement from the spectator to go anywhere beyond the immediate diegetic concern; it depends on action from outside. It is something of a cliché to define art cinema by its relative thoughtfulness in contrast to the mindless mainstream – this is certainly not what I am claiming here (many blockbuster films offer pause for thought and moments of ambiguity; many art films abide by a very formulaic linear storytelling tradition, heavily restricting spectatorial engagement). What makes the politics of authorship in *Climates* significant is its diverse, profoundly layered appeal to the spectator. A similar claim has been made by Angelo Restivo in his discussion of *The Conformist* (Bernardo Bertolucci, 1970). Distinguishing his approach from the 'hermeneutics of suspicion' (Restivo 2010: 178), which he claims informs the methods of counter-cinema (and, it should be said, its accompanying film theories), *The Conformist* produces a tension between 'a semiotic project, and the body traversed by all sorts of destabilizing pulsions' (ibid.: 172). Drawing on Lyotard as well as a range of other aesthetic theories, Restivo argues that the film contains 'the creative force of deformation' (ibid.: 176). By simply destabilising the apparent import of an image's narrative meaning, one can discover the seed of figuration, which might lead to new ways of seeing and thinking. While he does not do so explicitly, he at least implicitly grants the political potential of art cinema to the spectator, arguing that the 'extent to which any moving-image work . . . is judged to be political would then depend upon the extent to which the plastics of the image induces the kind of discord that is productive of new thought' (ibid.: 178). I agree with Restivo on this point: it is not the thoughtfulness, but the production of *new thought* arising from that encounter which has the potential to excite political activity.

The production of new thought arising from a discord between form and content can certainly be linked to *The Nine Muses*, too. The significance of Akomfrah's work, however, regards not only certain unforeseen political possibilities. Rather, disrupting the apparent divide that separates a politics of aesthetics or and aesthetics of politics, the foreignness of *The Nine Muses* defines equally the way one frames a social narrative and the formal approach. The foreigner of Akomfrah's work is as much the product of interlacing intermedial spaces as it is the historical body of post-imperial Britain. Rancière's aesthetic regime – which, I have argued, encompasses the discursive realm of art cinema – undermines hierarchies subordinating the merely cinematic to the intermedial or multimedial.

However, while we might accept the shared mode of aesthetic experience across media, and while the number of technologies utilised alone may not enhance the political substance of each text, the centrality of interconnecting media forms cannot simply be disregarded. Thus, while the egalitarian motivation of Rancière's aesthetic regime allows us to approach *any* text from the same starting point (potentially endowing *any* text with some unforeseen political potential), it offers little for analysis of works like *The Nine Muses*, preoccupied as they may be in the relationship between history and media forms. The socio-historical context is bound so determinedly and convolutedly to the formal language and technological diversity, to simply fall into line with the anti-specificity argument does a disservice to Akomfrah's effort. Akomfrah's fragmentation of forms and technologies is testament to this fact: a multitude of forms are brought together for shared purposes, with no one form given precedence over another. While it is questionable whether the tableau represents the best heterogeneous form – over, say, the jump cut (highlighting film's materiality and closeness to other material forms) or the long shot (highlighting a naturalistic convention that aligns cinema with a rich history of art) – *The Nine Muses* demonstrates how art cinema's stylistic heterogeneity can be linked to an ethics of heterogeneity. This might, in turn, come to shape a politics of heterogeneity, which is precisely the kind of claim I am attempting to make about art cinema in general. Taking further Galt and Schoonover's claim that the 'lack of strict parameters for art cinema . . . is as productive to film culture as it is frustrating to taxonomy' (Galt and Schoonover 2010: 7), art cinema's often overtly discursive relationship with the other arts becomes a way of enacting a political strategy of foreignness in Akomfrah's film.

This foregrounding of grand narratives on art history highlights the discursive constructedness of aesthetic hierarchies, the kind which are dismantled throughout each of the films I have discussed. To dismantle an artistic hierarchy while challenging an historiographical hierarchy (determining whose stories are told and how), in the even-handed manner of *The Nine Muses,* is to at once realise the terms of Rancière's 'political art' (Rancière 2004: 63) and undermine his claim that 'there is no politics of cinema' (Rancière 2014b: 104). Reinforcing the primary conviction of this thesis, contemporary art cinema like *The Nine Muses* antagonises consensus politics' key principle: 'that there is no more than what there is' (2010: xiii). Indeed, by pursuing the possibility of a political art cinema, *The Nine Muses* demonstrates, I think, that cinema potentialises even more than Rancière himself lets on.

Throughout this book, it has been my aim both to elucidate the political aesthetic theories of Rancière in relation to cinema and to challenge his limiting perspective of cinema as restricted to illustrations of political activity.

Instead, I have argued that art cinema offers a space of political potential through its open invitation to spectators, offering us the chance to convene and interrupt the existing social distribution. I have, therefore, defined political art cinema through its concern with interrupting dominant modes of perception, with a view to constructing a more inclusive site of participation. With this definition in mind, I shall bring together some of the recurring themes that could conceivably name a *contemporary political art cinema.*

In *The New Face of Political Cinema* (2007), Martin O'Shaughnessy has defined a similar domain through contrast with earlier forms of political cinema:

> Post-1968 film was able to feed off and prolong a vibrant radical politics. Contemporary political film is condemned to work in a very different context. It must seek to exist productively somewhere in the difficult space between the politics that was and an emergent new politics. While some have seen in it above all the shadow of a defeat and condemned it for its alleged political inadequacy, it is more interesting and more productive to assess it in terms of the effectiveness of the resistances that it mounts and its capacity to prepare the grounds for an emergent new politics. (O'Shaughnessy 2007: 2)

For O'Shaughnessy, the possibility of political cinema today is contingent upon shrugging off past defeats, recognising new challenges and remaining attentive to mounting resistance in these new sites of dissent. Contemporary political cinema, then, is determined by its concern for current social issues. Since what I have termed a 'politics of cinema' need not 'inscribe disagreement within . . . narratives, soundtracks and mise-en-scene', the films cannot, for O'Shaughnessy, be conceived of as 'political in a real sense' (ibid.: 180). Without a frame of critique that broaches a contemporary society in a clearly intelligible manner, such films lack the capacity to prepare grounds for an emergent new politics. Thus, while also turning to Rancière to make his claim, O'Shaughnessy and I arrive at different conclusions in terms of what constitutes political cinema today. For O'Shaughnessy, the 'effectiveness of the resistances' mounted by contemporary political films relates to their (1) 'capacity to puncture neoliberalism's utopian claims', (2) 'to bring socio-economic barriers to light' and (3) to 'assert the defiant right of those at the bottom to change social and physical locations' (ibid.: 181). O'Shaughnessy has supplemented Rancière's abstract philosophy of disagreement with contexts relating to the present in order to determine contemporary political cinema according to present-day social regimes, barriers and locations. This is an appropriate way of accounting for the films in his discussion, providing an exemplary understanding of the relationship between film and society today.

However, by necessitating representation of the contemporary socio-historical climate in the narrative, the characters are at a loss 'to reach outside the narrow spatial frame': just like real life, these films are 'unable to feed off a totalizing discourse of opposition, they cannot propose either a global critique or a global alternative' (ibid.). O'Shaughnessy's contemporary political cinema is confined to the real in ways that obstruct projection of a people yet to come.

Using Rancière's theories and arriving at a conclusion entirely the converse of O'Shaughnessy's, Davide Panagia has argued that cinema contains a political potential due to its essential, ontological nature of shock and interruption. Channelling the early film theory of Hugo Münsterberg, the moving image provides an 'assembly of disconnected movement in space and time that is compressed in such a way, and at such a speed, to offer us a sense of concerted movement' (Panagia 2013: 9). The ability of films to convey discontinuity within the apparently continuous is political, due to each film's 'rendering palpable of an interruption' (ibid.). Political cinema is not, then, determined by a concern for contemporary social issues for Panagia, but rather through 'a shock to subjectivity rather than a gateway to political subjugation' (ibid.) For Panagia, politics is entirely a matter of aesthetics; or, more precisely, of sensation. Social change brought about in and through cinema, then, depends on the extent to which films make 'explicit the fact of discontinuity in our political lives by giving privilege to the potentiality of non-necessity as a condition of existence' (Panagia 2013: 20). Unlike O'Shaughnessy, then, Panagia's argument would seem to define contemporary political cinema according to 'politics of cinema' model at the expense of a 'cinema of politics'. However, by privileging either the form or content of representation in the debate about how cinema is defined as political, we risk ignoring the nuances many films contain that traverse the harsh divide between aesthetic experience and historical representation. Contemporary political art cinema can be located on this threshold.

I do, however, share with both O'Shaughnessy and Panagia the view that the work undertaken by contemporary political art cinema regards the engagement of spectators. In this sense, I would agree that these films provide 'the grounds for an emergent new politics' (O'Shaughnessy 2007: 2) and spaces for 'elaborating ideas . . . not reducible to the analytics of argument' (Panagia 2013: 5). Prioritising neither a preferred subject or style, the heterogeneous category of political art cinema offers a broadly diverse mode of political engagement to a perpetually expanding field of spectators.

In a similar sense, William Brown has argued that contemporary political films might be wholly defined through this contesting of existing social and aesthetic paradigms. Broaching two stylistically different films – *Elite Squad* (José Padilha, 2007) and *A Screaming Man* (Mahamat Saleh Haroun, 2010) – Brown argues towards a tendency for contemporary political films to complicate division between movement and stasis in cinema, which Deleuze (1985) apportioned into the 'movement-image' and the 'time-image'. I discussed the complication of this division in some detail with regards to *No*, arguing that a relationship of ambivalence with existing political narratives offers a space of political potential. Brown argues that contemporary political cinema can be defined as 'a critique of passivity and a return to action' (Brown 2015: 163), suggesting that a tendency is emerging in contemporary political cinema for more explicit commitment to social causes. Reading through my analyses, one may be forgiven for questioning this location of action in contemporary political cinema. We have seen gestures indicating confinement, scepticism, madness, self-deprecation and disorientation, but outright expressions of antagonism appear few and far between. However, just as Brown's apposite example demonstrates, in the words of Aimé Césaire, 'a screaming man is not a dancing bear' (2001). Even inarticulate sounds break passivity and fracture the consensual order. Political art cinema today appears to challenge the divide between passivity and action, demanding instead the acute attention of spectators to engage with interruptive gestures and consider what role they might play.

What of political art cinema at a time of radical shifts to the right in the Western world? In my introduction, I claimed that the twenty-first-century far right represents an intensification of the consensual 'matching of sense with sense'. This may account for the way an 'ethical turn' has founded 'an unprecedented dramaturgy of infinite evil, justice and reparation' (Rancière 2010: 185), but can it account for its effects? Can these cinematic responses to consensus provide strategies for dealing with a global stage that hosts desperate escapes from the southern hemisphere to the north? Or the reconstruction of previously dismantled borders to prevent refuge? Or the intensification of immaterial borders separating the rich and the poor through the reaffirmation of global capitalism? Surely the foreignness of Akomfrah has never been more vital. At a time of global terror and persistently fascistic surveillance strategies, perhaps the effort urged by Panahi has become even more demanding. Our ability to image new worlds in the vein of Kaufman becomes even more compelling. As does the need for those in power to perform egalitarian gestures in the mode of Ceylan. Most crucial, perhaps, is this question of ambivalence, in the mode of Larraín: for how long can one remain critical of actions before a cause is clearly embraced?

Similarly, in a non-thematic sense, I have followed Rancière in the claim that, for art to be political, a paradox must emerge between the readability of a political message and an uncanny effect that disrupts clearly intelligible meaning. One would imagine, at times of social crises on a global scale, both the articulation of a message and the thwarting of that message brings new challenges to art filmmakers. Art films have historically worked in this gap between the clear and the unclear, using stylistic heterogeneity to complicate the conditions of our reality. At a time when clear political antagonism is arguably becoming more urgent, or desirable, or, for Brown, apparent, how do political art films remain art cinema-like? Does it instead shift to what Paola Marrati has termed the 'action-image': 'a cinematographic device [that] spells out the continuity of individual and collective ways of understanding social and historical life as oriented *by* and *toward* action' (2008: xii)? Panagia has argued that cinema, generally, is indicative of the action-image's embodiment of 'the modern political concern with rendering action visible' (2013: 9).

One must, I think, remain sceptical of straightforward matching of clearly visible action with political activity. Consider, for a moment, how much of what is socially and aesthetically reconfigurative in the history of art has relied on the prohibition of action and the veiling of clearly determined meaning. Similarly, while political art cinema might more clearly articulate the name of its opposition, we need not circumscribe the inactive. After all, it is inactivity that defines politics, for Rancière. Politics is described variously as disruptive, interruptive, that it 'occurs when . . . mechanisms are stopped in their tracks' (Rancière 1999: 17). Those looking to dissect the politics of tomorrow's political art films would do well to appreciate moments of stasis as much as action. Art cinema is defined by this fundamental embrace of stylistic and thematic heterogeneity; as such, political art cinema will continue to roam freely in varying aesthetic modes.

I have tried to account for the diversity of ways that art films construct spaces for the staging of politics. Irrespective of the new challenges posed at the time of writing, the question that informs tomorrow's political art films will remain: *to whom do these films speak?* Whilst the policing measures and exclusionary parameters of today's distributions of the sensible may become more intense or creative, the populations spoken to by these films might, in turn, change. This question of reception is complicated further by the changing technologies of viewing, new spaces of exhibition and emerging forms of spectatorship. The politics of art cinema is itself an area under discursive construction, with much still to learn.

NOTES

1. The assignment of *This is Not a Film* to any of these alternative categories would not discount the relevance of any of these elements. Nor would it prohibit the film's classification as an art film.
2. Greenblatt (1987).
3. See Diken (2008).
4. As I have explored in detail elsewhere (Harvey-Davitt 2016).

Bibliography

Abeel, Erica (2011) [original interview 2008], 'Charlie Kaufman on Synecdoche, New York', *Indiewire*, July 2011, indiewire.com: <http://www.indiewire.com/article/from_the_iw_vaults_charlie_kaufman_on_synecdoche_new_york> (accessed 4 December 2013).

Abel, Richard (1987), *French Cinema: The First Wave, 1915–1929*, Princeton, NJ: Princeton University Press.

Adorno, Theodor (1983), *Prisms*, translated by S. Weber and S. Weber, Cambridge, MA: MIT Press.

Adorno, Theodor (1992), *Notes to Literature*, vol. 2, translated by S. Weber Nicholson, New York: Columbia University Press.

Adorno, Theodor and Max Horkheimer (1997), *Dialectic of Enlightenment*, translated by E. Jephcott, London and New York: Verso.

Althusser, Louis (1969), *For Marx*, translated by B. Brewster, London: Verso.

Althusser, Louis (1971), 'Ideology and ideological state apparatuses', in *Lenin and Philosophy and other Essays*, translated by B. Brewster, New York: Monthly Review Press, pp. 85–126.

Arendt, Hannah (1963), *Eichmann in Jerusalem: A Report on the Banality of Evil*, New York: Viking Press.

Balázs, Béla (2004), 'The face of man', in L. Braudy and M. Cohen (eds), *Film Theory and Criticism*, Oxford: Oxford University Press, pp. 315–21.

Banks, Julia (2010), 'The texture of distance: approaching Nuri Bilge Ceylan's *Distant*', Fipresci.org: <http://www.fipresci.org/undercurrent/issue_0609/banks_distant.htm> (accessed 23 July 2013).

Barthes, Roland (1977), 'The death of the author', in *Image, Music, Text*, translated by S. Heath, London: Fontana Press, pp. 142–8.

Baudrillard, Jean (1994), *Simulacra and Simulation*, translated by S. Glaser, Ann Arbor, MI: University of Michigan Press.

Baudry, Jean-Louis (1974), 'Ideological effects of the basic cinematographic apparatus', translated by A. Williams, *Film Quarterly*, 28: 2, 39–47.

Baumbach, Nico (2013), 'What does it mean to call a film art?', in P. Bowman (ed.), *Rancière and Film*, Edinburgh: Edinburgh University Press, pp. 20–33.

Bayat, Asef (2010), *Life as Politics: How Ordinary People Change the Middle East*, Stanford, CA: Stanford University Press.

Bazin, André (1967), *What is Cinema*, vol.1, translated by H. Gray, Berkeley and Los Angeles: University of California Press.

Benjamin, Walter (1968), 'The work of art in the age of mechanical reproduction', in *Illuminations*, translated by H. Zohn, New York: Random House.

Benjamin, Walter (1999), *The Arcades Project*, translated by H. Eiland and K. McLaughlan, Cambridge, MA and London: Harvard University Press.

Berger, John and Jean Mohr (1975), *A Seventh Man*, London: Verso.

Bohne, Luciana (1984), 'The discourse of narcissism in *L'Avventura*', *Film Criticism*, 9: 1, 17–24.

Bordwell, David (2002), 'The art cinema as a mode of film practice', in C. Fowler (ed.), *The European Cinema Reader*, London: Routledge, pp. 94–102.

Bordwell, D. and K. Thompson (2010), *Film Art: An Introduction*, 7th edn, New York: McGraw-Hill.

Bowman, Paul and Richard Stamp (eds) (2011), *Reading Rancière: Critical Dissensus*, London and New York: Continuum.

Brown, William (2015), 'Contemporary political cinema: the impossibility of passivity', in E. Mazierska and L. Kristensen (eds), *Marxism and Film Activism: Screening Alternative Worlds*, New York and Oxford: Berghahn Books.

Buckland, Warren (2008), *Puzzle Films: Complex Storytelling in Contemporary Cinema*, London: Wiley-Blackwell.

Butler, Alison (2010), 'A deictic turn: space and location in contemporary gallery film and video installation', *Screen*, 51: 4, 305–23.

Césaire, Aimé (2001), *Notebook of a Return to a Native Land*, translated by C. Eshleman and A. Smith, Middletown, CT: Wesleyan University Press.

Chambers, Samuel A. (2013), *The Lessons of Rancière*, Durham, NC: Duke University Press.

Chaudhuri, S. and H. Finn (2003), 'The open image: poetic realism and the New Iranian Cinema', *Screen*, 44: 1, 38–57.

Citton, Yves (2009), 'Political ambivalence and the agency of the sensible', in G. Rockhill and P. Watts (eds), *Jacques Rancière: History, Politics, Aesthetics*, Durham, NC: Duke University Press.

Cohen, Joshua (2010), *Rousseau: A Free Community of Equals*, Oxford: Oxford University Press.

Comolli, Jean-Luc and Paul Narboni (1971), 'Cinema/ideology/criticism', in *Screen Reader 1: Cinema/Ideology/Politics*, London: SEFT, pp. 2–11.

Conley, Tom (2009), 'Fabulation and contradiction: Jacques Rancière on cinema', in T. Trifonova (ed.), *European Film Theory*, New York and Abingdon: Routledge.

Dabashi, Hamid (2001), *Close Up: Iranian Cinema, Past, Present, and Future*, New York: Verso.

Deleuze, Gilles (1985), *Cinema 2: The Time Image*, Minneapolis: University of Minnesota.

Deming, Richard (2011), 'Living a part: *Synecdoche, New York*, metaphor, and the problem of scepticism', in David La Rocca (ed.), *The Philosophy of Charlie Kaufman*, Lexington: University Press of Kentucky.

Diken, Bülent (2008), 'Climates of nihilism', *Third Text*, 22: 6, 719–32.

Doane, Mary Ann (2003), 'The close-up: scale and detail in the cinema', *differences: A Journal of Feminist Cultural Studies*, 14: 3, 89–111.

Dönmez-Colin, Gönül (2008), *Turkish Cinema: Identity, Distance, Belonging*, London: Reaktion Books.

Dyer, Geoff (2012), *Zona: A Book About a Film About a Journey to a Room*, Edinburgh: Canongate.

Elder, R. Bruce (2006), *Image and Identity: Reflections on Canadian Film and Culture*, Ontario: Wilfrid Laurier University Press.

Elsaesser, Thomas (2005), *European Cinema: Face to Face With Hollywood*, Amsterdam: Amsterdam University Press.

Elsaesser, Thomas (2009), 'The mind-game film', in W. Buckland (ed.), *Puzzle Films: Complex Storytelling in Contemporary Cinema*, Chichester: Wiley-Blackwell, pp. 13–41.

Foucault, Michel (1975), *Discipline and Punish*, translated by A. Sheridan, New York: Random House.

Foucault, Michel (1986), 'What is an author?', *The Foucault Reader*, translated by P. Rabinow, London: Penguin, pp. 101–20.

Foucault, Michel (2008), *The Birth of Biopolitics: Lectures at the Collège de France, 1978–1979*, translated by G. Burchell, London: Palgrave Macmillan.

Fowler, Catherine (2004), 'Room for experiment: gallery films and vertical time from Maya Deren to Eija Liisa Ahtila', *Screen*, 45: 4, 324–43.

Frye, Northrop (1957), *The Anatomy of Criticism*, Princeton, NJ: Princeton University Press.

Fukuyama, Francis (1992), *The End of History and The Last Man*, London: Penguin.

Galt, Rosalind and Karl Schoonover (2010), 'Introduction: the impurity of art cinema', in R. Galt and K. Schoonover (eds), *Global Art Cinema: New Theories and Histories*, Oxford: Oxford University Press.

Giovacchini, S. and R. Sklar (eds) (2012), *Global Neorealism: The Transnational History of a Film Style*, Jackson: University Press of Mississippi.

Greenberg, Clement (1990), 'Modernist painting', in J. Thompson (ed.), *Twentieth Century Theories of Art*, Ottawa: Carleton University Press, pp. 94–101.

Greenblatt, Stephen (1987), 'Towards a poetics of culture', *Southern Review*, 20: 1, 3–15.

Griffin, Dustin (2015), *Satire: A Critical Reintroduction*, Lexington: University Press of Kentucky.

Hallward, Peter (2006b), 'Staging equality: on Rancière's theatocracy', *New Left Review*, 37, January–February, 109–29.

Harvey, David (2005), *A Brief History of Neoliberalism*, Oxford: Oxford University Press.

Harvey, Sylvia (1982), 'Whose Brecht? Memories for the eighties', *Screen*, 23: 1, 45–59.

Harvey-Davitt, James (2014), 'Disputing Rossellini: three French perspectives', *NECSUS: European Journal of Media Studies*, 3: 2, 63–80.

Harvey-Davitt, James (2016), 'Conflicted selves: the humanist cinema of Nuri Bilge Ceylan', *New Review of Film and Television Studies*, 14: 2, 249–67.

Hegel, Georg Wilhelm Friedrich [1820] (2008), *Outlines of the Philosophy of Right*, translated by T. M. Knox, Oxford: Oxford University Press.

Hoby, Hermione (2009), 'The ultimate postmodern novel is a film', *The Guardian*, Wednesday 13 May 2009, <http://www.theguardian.com/books/booksblog/2009/may/13/synecdoche-postmodern-novel-film> (accessed 5 December 2013).

Hugo, Victor [1831] (1978), *Notre Dame de Paris*, translated by J. Sturrock, London and New York: Penguin Classics.

Jacobs, Steven (2011), *Framing Pictures: Film and the Visual Arts*, Edinburgh: Edinburgh University Press.

Jameson, Fredric (1991), *Postmodernism, or, The Cultural Logic of Late Capitalism*, Durham, NC: Duke University Press.

Jones, Jeffrey P. (2010), *Entertaining Politics: Satiric Television and Political Engagement*, Plymouth: Rowman and Littlefield Publishers Inc.

Kafka, Franz (1925), *The Trial*, Berlin: Verlag die Schmiede.

Kant, Immanuel [1790] (2000), *Critique of Judgement*, translated by J. C. Meredith, Oxford: Oxford University Press.

Kilbourn, Russell J. A. (2013), *Cinema, Memory, Modernity: The Representation of Memory from the Art Film to Transational Cinema*, London: Routledge.

Klawans, Stuart (2004), 'Styles of radical will', *The Nation*, 4 October 2004, New York, p. 32.

Koutsourakis, Angelos (2013), *Politics as Form in Lars von Trier: A Post-Brechtian Reading*, London and New York: Bloomsbury.

Landy, Marcia (1996), *Cinematic Uses of the Past*, Minneapolis: University of Minnesota Press.

Landy, Marcia (2015), *Cinema and Counter History*, Bloomington: Indiana University Press.

Lyttelton, Oliver (2013), 'Interview: director Pablo Larrain on the unique aesthetic of 'No' & working with star Gael García Bernal', *Indiewire*, 12 February 2013, <http://blogs.indiewire.com/theplaylist/interview-director-pablo-larrain-on-the-unique-aesthetic-of-no-working-with-star-gael-García-bernal-20130212> (accessed 27 March 2014).

MacCabe, Colin (1985), *Theoretical Essays: Film, Linguistics, Literature*, Manchester: Manchester University Press.

McKim, Kristi (2013), *Cinema as Weather: Stylistic Screens and Atmospheric Change*, London: Routledge.

Maltby, Richard (2003), *Hollywood Cinema*, Malden and Oxford: Wiley-Blackwell.

Marrati, Paola (2008), *Gilles Deleuze: Cinema and Philosophy*, Baltimore, MD: Johns Hopkins University Press.

Marx, Karl and Friedrich Engels [1848] (2004), *The Communist Manifesto*, London: Penguin.

Masters, Roger D. (1968), *The Political Philosophy of Rousseau*, Princeton, NJ: Princeton University Press.

May, Todd (2008), *The Political Thought of Jacques Rancière: Creating Equality*, Edinburgh: Edinburgh University Press.

Mayne, Judith (1993), *Cinema and Spectatorship*, London and New York: Routledge.

Mondloch, Kate (2010), *Screens: Viewing Media Installation Art*, Minneapolis: University of Minnesota Press.

Morgan, Daniel (2006), 'Rethinking Bazin: ontology and realist aesthetics', *Critical Inquiry*, 32, Spring 2006, 443–81.

Mulvey, Laura (1975), 'Visual pleasure and narrative cinema', *Screen*, 16: 3, 6–18.

Münsterberg, Hugo (2002), *Hugo Münsterberg on Film: The Photoplay – a Psychological Study and Other Writings*, ed. A. Langdale, New York and London: Routledge.

Neale, Steve (1981), 'Art cinema as institution', *Screen*, 22: 1, 11–40.

Nichols, Bill (1991), *Representing Reality: Issues and Concepts in Documentary*, Bloomington: Indiana University Press.

O'Shaughnessy, Martin (2007), *The New Face of Political Cinema: Commitment in French Film Since 1995*, New York and Oxford: Berghahn.

Panagia, Davide (2013), 'Why film matters to political theory', *Contemporary Political Theory*, 12: 1, 2–25.

Paul, Ian Alan (2010), 'Desiring-machines in American cinema: what *Inception* tells us about our experience of reality and film', *Senses of Cinema*, October 2010, <http://sensesofcinema.com/2010/feature-articles/desiring-machines-in-american-cinema-what-inception-tells-us-about-our-experience-of-reality-and-film/> (accessed 5 December 2013).

Peucker, Brigitte (2007), *The Material Image: Art and the Real in Film*, Stanford, CA: Stanford University Press.

Pisters, Patricia (2012), *The Neuro-Image: A Deleuzian Filmphilosophy of Digital Screen Culture*. Stanford, CA: Stanford University Press.

Rancière, Jacques (1991), *The Ignorant Schoolmaster: Five Lessons in Intellectual Emancipation*, translated by K. Ross, Stanford, CA: Stanford University Press.

Rancière, Jacques (1992), 'Politics, identification, and subjectivization', in *October 61*, Summer 1992, 58–64.

Rancière, Jacques (1994), *The Names of History*, translated by H. Melehy, Minneapolis: University of Minnesota Press.

Rancière, Jacques (1999), *Disagreement: Politics and Philosophy*, translated by J. Rose, Minneapolis: Minnesota University Press.

Rancière, Jacques (2003), *Short Voyages to the Land of the People*, translated by J. B. Swenson, Stanford, CA: Stanford University Press.

Rancière, Jacques (2004), *The Politics of Aesthetics*, translated by G. Rockhill, New York: Continuum.

Rancière, Jacques (2006a), *Film Fables*, translated by E. Batista, London : Berg.

Rancière, Jacques (2006b), *Hatred of Democracy*, translated by S. Corcoran, London and New York : Verso.

Rancière, Jacques (2007), *The Future of the Image*, translated by G. Elliot, London and New York: Verso.

Rancière, Jacques (2009a), *Aesthetics and its Discontents*, translated by S. Corcoran, Cambridge: Polity Press.

Rancière, Jacques (2009b), *The Aesthetic Unconscious*, translated by J. Rose, Cambridge and Malden: Polity Press.

Rancière, Jacques (2009c), *The Emancipated Spectator*, translated by G. Elliot, London and New York: Verso.

Rancière, Jacques (2010), *Dissensus: On Politics and Aesthetics*, translated by S. Corcoran, London and New York: Continuum.

Rancière, Jacques (2011a), *Althusser's Lesson*, translated by E. Batista, London and New York: Continuum.

Rancière, Jacques (2011b), *Mute Speech*, translated by J. Swenson, New York: Columbia University Press.

Rancière, Jacques (2013), *Aisthesis: Scenes from the Aesthetic Regime of Art*, translated by Z. Paul, London and New York: Verso.

Rancière, Jacques (2014a), *Figures of History*, translated by J. Rose, Cambridge: Polity Press.

Rancière, Jacques (2014b), *The Intervals of Cinema*, translated by J. Howe, London and New York: Verso.

Ray, Gene (2004), 'Conditioning Adorno', *Third Text*, 18: 4, 223–30.

Rees, A. L. (1999), *A History of Experimental Film and Video*, London: Palgrave Macmillan.

Restivo, Angelo (2010), 'From index to figure in the European art film: the case of *The Conformist*', in R. Galt and K. Schoonover (eds), *Global Art Cinema: New Theories and Histories*, Oxford: Oxford University Press, pp. 164–80.

Robson, Mark (2013), 'Cinemarxis: Rancière and Godard', in P. Bowman (ed.), *Rancière and Film*, Edinburgh: Edinburgh University Press, pp. 133–48.

Rockhill, Gabriel (2004), 'Appendix I: Glossary of technical terms', in J. Rancière, *The Politics of Aesthetics*, New York: Continuum.

Rodowick, D. N. (1994), *The Crisis of Political Modernism: Criticism and Ideology in Contemporary Film Theory*, Berkeley and Los Angeles: University of California Press.

Rohter, Larry (2013), 'One prism on the undoing of Pinochet', *New York Times*, 8 February 2013, <http://www.nytimes.com/2013/02/10/movies/oscar-nominated-no-stirring-debate-in-chile.html?pagewanted=all&_r=2&> (accessed 20 March 2013).

Rosen, Philip (2001), *Change Mummified: Cinema, Historicity, Theory*, Minneapolis: University of Minnesota Press.

Ross, Kristin (2002), *May '68 and Its Afterlives*, London and Chicago: University of Chicago Press.

Roth, Philip (1997), *American Pastoral*, London: Vintage.

Rousseau, Jean-Jacques [1762] (2008), *The Social Contract*, translated by M. Cranston, Oxford: Oxford University Press.

Rushton, Richard (2013), *The Politics of Hollywood Cinema*, New York: Palgrave Macmillan.

Schiller, Friedrich [1794] (2004), *On the Aesthetic Education of Man*, translated by R. Snell, Mineola, NY: Dover Publications.

Sconce, Jeffrey (2002), 'Irony, nihilism and the new American "smart" film', *Screen*, 43: 4, pp. 349–69.

Shachar, Hila (2013), 'Authorial histories: the historical film and the literary biopic', in R. Rosenstone and C. Parvalescu (eds), *A Companion to the Historical Film*, Chichester: Wiley-Blackwell, pp. 199–218.

Sharits, Paul (1978), 'Statement regarding multiple screen/sound "locational" film environments – installations', *Film Culture*, 65–6, 78–9.

Shaviro, Steven (1995), 'Two lessons from Burroughs', in J. M. Halberstam and I. Livingston (eds), *Posthuman Bodies*, Indianapolis: Indiana University Press.

Sitney, P. Adams (1974), *Visionary Film: The American Avant-Garde, 1943–2000*, Oxford and New York: Oxford University Press.

Suner, Asuman (2004), 'Horror of a different kind: dissonant voices of a new Turkish cinema', *Screen*, 45: 4, 305–23.

Thompson, Kristin (1985), 'From primitive to classical', in *The Classical Hollywood Cinema: Film Mode and Style of Production to 1960*, London: Routledge, pp. 245–64.

Tweedie, James (2013), *The Age of New Waves: Art Cinema And The Staging Of Globalization*, Oxford: Oxford University Press.

Weinberger, Stephen (2007), 'Neorealism, Iranian style', *Iranian Studies*, 40: 1, 5–16.

Wheatley, Catherine (2009), *Michael Haneke's Cinema: The Ethic of the Image*, New York and Oxford: Berghahn Books.

White, Hayden (1973), *Metahistory: The Historical Imagination in Nineteenth-Century Europe*, Baltimore, MD: Johns Hopkins University Press.

Willinsky, Barbara (2001), *Sure Seaters: The Emergence of Art House Cinemas*, Minneapolis: University of Minnesota Press.

Wood, Robin (2006), 'Climates and other disasters', *Artforum International*, 45, 3 November 2006, pp. 284–6.

Filmography

À ma Soeur! (France, Catherine Breillat, 2001)
A Screaming Man (France, Belgium, Chad, Mahamat Saleh Haroun, 2010)
A Star is Born (USA, William Wellman, 1937)
Adaptation (USA, Spike Jonze, 2002)
Amores Perros (Mexico, Alejandro González Iñárritu, 2000)
Being John Malkovich (USA, Spike Jonze, 1999)
Bicycle Thieves (Italy, Vittorio De Sica, 1948)
Black Girl (Senegal, France, Ousmane Sembene, 1966)
Buried (USA, Spain, France, Rodrigo Cortés, 2010)
Central Station (Brazil, France, Walter Salles, 1998)
Climates (Turkey, France, Nuri Bilge Ceylan, 2006)
Closed Curtain (Iran, Jafar Panahi, 2013)
Colossal Youth (Portugal, France, Switzerland, Pedro Costa, 2006)
Crimson Gold (Iran, Jafar Panahi, 2003)
Daisies (Czechoslovakia, Věra Chytilová, 1966)
Distant (Turkey, Nuri Bilge Ceylan, 2002)
Dogville (Denmark, Sweden, France, Germany, Netherlands, Norway, Finland, Italy, Lars von Trier, 2003)
Elite Squad (Brazil, USA, Argentina, José Padilha, 2007)
Eternal Sunshine of the Spotless Mind (USA, Michel Gondry, 2004)
Europe '51 (Italy, Roberto Rossellini, 1952)
Fahrenheit 9/11 (USA, Michael Moore, 2004)
Five Broken Cameras (Palestine, Israel, France, Netherlands, Emad Burnat and Guy Davidi, 2011)
Funny Games (Austria, Michael Haneke, 1997)
Gone With the Wind (USA, Victor Fleming, 1939)
Handsworth Songs (UK, Black Audio Film Collective, 1987)
Hidden (France, Austria, Germany, Italy, USA, Michael Haneke, 2005)
Histoire(s) du Cinéma (France, Switzerland, Jean-Luc Godard, 1989–99)
Ikiru (Japan, Akira Kurosawa, 1952)
Irreversible (France, Gaspar Noé, 2002)
Jeanne Dielman, 23, Quai du Commerce, 1080 Bruxelles (Belgium, Chantal Akerman, 1975)

Joy of Madness (Afghanistan, Iran, Hana Makhmalbaf, 2003)
L'Avventura (Italy, France, Michelangelo Antonioni, 1960)
La Chinoise (France, Jean-Luc Godard, 1967)
La Grande Illusion (France, Jean Renoir, 1937)
Le Temps de Vivre (France, Bernard Paul, 1969)
Les Misérables (USA, UK, Tom Hooper, 2012)
Listen to Britain (UK, Humphrey Jennings, 1942)
Machuca (Chile, Spain, UK, France, Andrés Wood, 2004)
Mad Men (USA, Matthew Weiner, 2007–15)
Memories of Underdevelopment (Chile, Tomás Gutiérrez Alea, 1968)
Missing (USA, Costa-Gavras, 1982)
Mystic River (USA, Australia, Clint Eastwood, 2003)
No (Chile, USA, France, Mexico, Pablo Larraín, 2012)
Nostalgia for the Light (Chile, France, Germany, Spain, USA, Patricio Guzmán, 2010)
Performance (UK, Donald Cammell and Nicolas Roeg, 1970)
Post Mortem (Chile, Germany, Mexico, Pablo Larraín, 2010)
Red Desert (Italy, France, Michelangelo Antonioni, 1964)
Rome, Open City (Italy, Roberto Rossellini, 1945)
Safe (USA, Todd Haynes, 1995)
Sátántangó (Hungary, Béla Tarr, 1994)
Soy Cuba (Cuba, Soviet Union, Mikhail Kalatozov, 1964)
Spartacus (USA, Stanley Kubrick, 1960)
Stalker (Soviet Union, Andrei Tarkovsky, 1979)
Synecdoche, New York (USA, Charlie Kaufman, 2008)
Taxi (Iran, Jafar Panahi, 2015)
The Circle (Iran, Jafar Panahi, 2000)
The Conformist (Iran, Bernardo Bertolucci, 1970)
The Edge of Love (UK, John Maybury, 2008)
The General Line (Soviet Union, Sergei Eisenstein, 1929)
The Mirror (Iran, Jafar Panahi, 1997)
The Motorcycle Diaries (Argentina, USA, Chile, Peru, Brazil, UK, Germany, France, Walter Salles, 2004)
The Nine Muses (Ghana, UK, John Akomfrah, 2010)
The Passion of Joan of Arc (France, Carl Theodor Dreyer, 1928)
The Silence (Sweden, Ingmar Bergman, 1963)
The Sun (Russia, Italy, Switzerland, France, Aleksandr Sokurov, 2005)
The White Ribbon (Germany, Austria, France, Italy, Michael Haneke, 2009)
This is Not a Film (Iran, Jafar Panahi, 2011)
Tony Manero (Chile, Pablo Larraín, 2008)
Tout Va Bien (France, Jean-Luc Godard and Jean-Pierre Gorin, 1972)
Umberto D (Italy, Vittorio De Sica, 1952)
Way Down East (USA, D. W. Griffith, 1920)
White House Down (USA, Roland Emmerich, 2013)
Winter Sleep (Turkey, Germany, France, Nuri Bilge Ceylan, 2014)
Y Tu Mamá También (Mexico, Alfonso Cuarón, 2001)
Zero Dark Thirty (USA, Kathryn Bigelow, 2012)
Z (France, Algeria, Costa-Gavras, 1969)

Index

CPSIA information can be obtained
at www.ICGtesting.com
Printed in the USA
BVHW061554300620
582685BV00003B/32

9 781474 462938